THE FREEDOM OF OBEDIENCE

Other books in the Carthusian Novice Conferences series

The Way of Silent Love
The Call of Silent Love
Interior Prayer

CISTERCIAN STUDIES SERIES NUMBER ONE HUNDRED SEVENTY-TWO

THE FREEDOM OF OBEDIENCE

Carthusian Novice Conferences

by
a Carthusian

Translated by
an Anglican Solitary

Cistercian Publications
Kalamazoo, Michigan

First published in 1998 by
Darton, Longman and Todd Ltd
1 Spencer Court
140–2 Wandsworth High Street
London SW18 4JJ

and by

Cistercian Publications Inc.
Institute of Cistercian Studies
Western Michigan University
Kalamazoo, MI 49008
and
Saint Joseph's Abbey
Spencer, MA 01562

The work of Cistercian Publications is made possible in part by
support from Western Michigan University to The Institute of
Cistercian Studies

ISBN 0 87907 772 7

Phototypeset by Intype London Ltd
Printed and bound in Great Britain by
Redwood Books, Trowbridge, Wiltshire

Contents

Acknowledgements

Sr Maureen Scrine for her faithful work of correction, and a perfectionist young Carthusian monk.

1

The Freedom of Love

LIBERATION

Let us recall this essential truth: the ascetic aspect makes sense only in the measure that it leads to the flowering of the life of Christ in us.

> True, [as] the baptised Christian 'is dead to sin and dedicated to God; but desires to derive still more abundant fruit from the grace of baptism. For this purpose he makes profession in the Church of the evangelical counsels. He does so for two reasons: first, in order to be set free from hindrances that could hold him back from fervent charity and perfect worship of God, and secondly, in order to consecrate himself in a more thorough-going way to the service of God.'[1]

The practice of the evangelical counsels frees the monk from all that could hinder him in his quest for the fullness of love and perfect service of God. He renounces not only sin, but every tie, all that is superfluous – even of things that are good in themselves. Like a mountaineer faced with an ascent. Let us never forget that what he seeks is love.

> Whom have I in heaven but you?
> And having you I desire nothing upon earth.
> Though my flesh and my heart should waste away,
> God is the strength of my heart and my portion for ever.
>
> (Psalm 73:25–6)

STABLE COMMITMENT

'The bonds by which he pledges himself to the practice
of the counsels show forth the unbreakable bond of union
that exists between Christ and his bride the Church.'[2]

It is perpetual profession that most clearly manifests the
union between Christ and the Church, of which it is an
individual realisation. The constitution starts always with the
Church: it is she who is the Spouse of Christ. It is as
members of the Church that we are united to Christ. Consecration by means of vows creates a particular union with the
Lord in a spiritual intimacy which is and ought to be such
that it possesses in its own way the depth of conjugal union.
'But anyone united to the Lord becomes one spirit with him'
(1 Corinthians 6:17). We have here one of the profound
theological reasons for the permanent and indissoluble
character of religious commitment. The vow of love is to
give oneself totally, without reserve.

Human beings are fickle and capricious creatures, a breath
of air disturbs them. What they want today they are indifferent to tomorrow. When the flame of love burns brightly,
they want to consecrate themselves to the Lord. But in the
day of dryness and testing, in twenty years, who knows? And
yet, if their gift of self does not include their whole life, it is
not complete. Is it possible to give in advance, by an act of
will, that which doesn't already exist? Existentialist philo-
sophers, with their eye fixed on the spontaneity and truth of
the present moment, each moment taken separately, say no.
If in twenty years my interior dispositions don't correspond
any longer to the act that has been made, is this act false, a
lie? In addition, am I the same person that I was twenty
years ago? What is a person? Is it the transient centre of
stimuli and reactions in each present moment, without a link
to what has gone before or what follows after, or something
that endures throughout the changes of life?

For the Christian, the spiritual centre of the human person, the self, maintains its fundamental identity for the whole of life on earth, and is destined for participation in the eternal life of God. Through the application of his intelligence, the person can focus on transcendent values (truth, beauty, love, etc.) and rise above the flux of time. Through his liberty, he can choose the meaning and orientation that he will give to his life. He can bind himself in advance in order to realise this act, this good. In this case, his authenticity as a human person doesn't reside in conforming his emotions to what he does in the moment that he does it (that is to say, in the spontaneity of the act), but in conforming the act of this moment to the meaning and intent which he formerly chose to give it. The person is not a succession of separate points at the mercy of the conditions of the moment. God has given him to share in his power as creator, and to create himself through his liberty, to go beyond himself towards absolute values.

In making a vow, the person takes the most radical means of focusing his will in the good.

> The purpose of the vow is to establish the will in the good. And the acts which proceed from a will thus fixed in the good become perfect virtue.[3]

Let us be realistic and humble enough to realise that we have, and we will have, need of this support. It is the prudence of our believing and reasonable self that guards against the fragility and instability of our superficial and passionate self. Like the bond between Christ and his Church, our union with Christ will pass through moments of darkness, will grow according to laws that sometimes escape us. In these moments it is essential that our will be fastened ahead of time to the will of the Father in Christ. A wise person builds on a rock.

> I love you, O Lord my strength,
> O Lord my stronghold, my crag and my haven.
> My God, my rock in whom I put my trust,
> my shield, the horn of my salvation, and my refuge.
>
>   (Psalm 18:1–2)[4]

HAPPY NECESSITY

The obligation that we impose on ourselves by the vow doesn't contradict our liberty; it is rather its perfect expression. Because the essence of liberty is not the power to choose between good and evil but to do the good. We see this in the saints who are rooted in the good and are unable to do evil. On this subject, St Augustine says that it is a 'happy necessity that compels us to do a better thing.' And elsewhere he says, 'Don't regret your vows. On the contrary, rejoice that it is no longer permitted you to engage in harmful license.'[5]

> Before making a vow, prepare yourself;
> do not be like one who puts the Lord to the test.
> (Sirach 18:23)

We are free to make a vow or not to make it. Once made, we owe it to God and ourselves to fulfil it.

> 'If you make a vow to the Lord your God, do not postpone fulfilling it; for the Lord your God will surely require it of you, and you would incur guilt. But if you refrain from vowing, you will not incur guilt. Whatever your lips utter you must diligently perform, just as you have freely vowed to the Lord your God with your own mouth.'
> (Deuteronomy 23:21–4)

FROM THE UNKNOWN, TOWARDS THE UNKNOWN

When it is a question of a vow to perform an individual act, everything is, ordinarily, more simple. But here it is a question of the entire person and for the whole of life. The vow does not take away that part of the unknown that opens out before our freedom. On the one hand, we cannot have perfect interior certainty that God calls us. This re-echoes in our psyche, bringing into play intelligence, affectivity and will. The criteria aren't objective, but subjective. There is always a risk entailed; mathematical certainty isn't possible. To demand it is already to move outside of the human condition.

On the other hand, there is another unknown, what will come to be. The future living-out of what I promise is something that I can only know indirectly, abstractly, with the capacity for comprehension that corresponds to who I am, to my human and spiritual experience, here and now. This creates a particularly uncomfortable psychological situation. Extrapolation into the future is always more or less inaccurate. I have to make a plan – but I don't know how it will turn out. I must not get attached to its material details. More profoundly than on my purpose, I rely on the Lord. It is by walking towards him, by being constantly at the disposal of his will, in the poverty of my self, that I try more and more to be in harmony with that which he wants of me, with this Word who creates me unceasingly in the truth of the divine liberty.

Understand me! God does not contradict himself. What he calls me to today will be in continuity with that which I understood of his Word yesterday. It is by the hollowing out of fidelity that we are opened to liberty and love.

FOLLOWING CHRIST

Christ is the heart of religious life. From the beginning of *Perfectae Caritatis*, it is defined as following Christ.

> From the very beginning of the Church there were men and women who set out to follow Christ with greater liberty, and to imitate him more closely.[6]

The decree goes on to tell us that ' . . .the final norm of the religious life is the following of Christ as it is put before us in the Gospel, this must be taken by all institutes as the supreme rule.'[7] The constitutions of the various Orders are nothing but the application of the gospel from the point of view of the particular way each Order is called by the Spirit to follow Christ. We must never forget this. Our Statutes ought to be interpreted and lived according to the spirit of the gospel, and can never contradict it.

In the final analysis, the whole Church is the single perfect imitator of the incarnate Word, each particular vocation manifesting just one part of its riches, at least at the level of concrete realisation, each being animated by his Spirit and his love.

> Let religious see well to it that the Church truly show forth Christ through them with ever-increasing clarity to believers and unbelievers alike – Christ in contemplation on the mountain, or proclaiming the kingdom of God to the multitudes, or healing the sick and maimed and converting sinners to a good life, or blessing children and doing good to all men, always in obedience to the will of the Father who sent him.[8]

The practice of the evangelical counsels is a means that 'has the power to conform the Christian man more fully to that kind of poor and virginal life which Christ the Lord chose for himself and which his Virgin Mother embraced also.'[9]

The style of Christ's life orders the nature of the religious life, and is its *raison d'être* and supreme criterion; this demands a very special union with Christ.

All those who are called by God to the practice of the evangelical counsels, and who make faithful profession of them, consecrate themselves to the Lord in a special way. They follow Christ who, virginal and poor (cf. Mt. 8:20; Lk. 9:58), redeemed and sanctified men by obedience unto death on the cross (cf. Phil. 2:8). Under the impulse of love, which the Holy Spirit pours into their hearts (cf. Rom. 5:5), they live more and more for Christ and for his body, the Church (cf. Col. 1:24).[10]

TO LIVE THE GOSPEL IN ITS FULLNESS

The tradition has emphasised the counsels of obedience, poverty and chastity as the most important. Let us not forget that there are other counsels in the gospel: hospitality, hidden almsgiving, unceasing prayer, fraternal correction, prudent and detached use of the good things of this world, the relinquishing of one's own rights in the service of peace and love, the simplicity of a child, etc. The imitation of Christ is attached first of all to the person of Christ, to his example and to all his teaching. The three classical counsels (obedience, poverty and chastity) are three lines of strength, but they ought to be understood and lived in the light of the entire gospel, and in function of the love which is the ultimate goal. This is the great tradition. In Augustine's rule, for example, we find the ideal of a life in unity of soul and heart in God through poverty, simplicity, humility, prayer, fasting, chastity, modesty, obedience, fraternal correction, the pardoning of offences. The rule of St Benedict is yet more flexible, grouping together in chapter IV seventy-four precepts which comprise traits that correspond to the whole teaching of the gospel. The pattern for religious is quite simply to live the gospel in its fullness.

The three counsels are the privileged (but not exclusive) means that allow for greater responsiveness[11] to the activity of the Spirit. Christ himself, through the Spirit, inscribes his image on those who generously work on their hearts, make themselves poor in themselves and put themselves at the disposal of grace. The imitation of Christ isn't copying an exterior model, but a more and more complete inscribing in the baptised of the reality of Easter, implanted in us by baptism and fed by the Eucharist. At the heart of this life in us is the attitude of complete fidelity to and communion with the Father which was that of Christ. From the first moment of his life, from ' "See, God, I have come to do your will . . ." ' (Hebrews 10:7) until the last moment, ' "Father, into your hands I commend my spirit" ' (Luke 23:46) the life of Jesus was a perfect gift of self, a total sacrifice in love, to the Father and to us all.

IN AND FOR THE CHURCH

Being means to and instruments of love, the evangelical counsels unite those who practise them to the Church and her mystery in a special way. It follows that the spiritual life of such Christians should be dedicated also to the welfare of the entire Church. To the extent of their capacities and in keeping with the particular kind of religious life to which they are individually called, whether it be one of prayer or of active labour as well they have the duty of working for the implanting and strengthening of the kingdom of Christ in souls and for spreading it to the four corners of the earth.[12]

The will to live the gospel fully unites us to the entire Church and excludes any parochialism. We ought to open ourselves to its life, which is the life of the Spirit, to its needs and preoccupations. Christian life is a life of love, therefore necessarily apostolic. This apostolic charity is expressed by each according to the form of his own vocation, therefore, for us, essentially by prayer and penance.

In being, for the members of the Church, the sign that we have here below no lasting city, that we are in search of the city to come, the religious state ought also to manifest 'more clearly to all believers the heavenly goods which are already present in this age, witnessing to the new and eternal life which we have acquired through the redemptive work of Christ and preluding our future resurrection and the glory of the heavenly kingdom.'[13] The religious is witness to the transcendent dimension of the kingdom of God, whereas the laity witnesses to its immanence in the world. The entire Church is the 'lumen gentium', the sign for the world of the salvation of God. The religious state takes this aspect of its life to the highest intensity, and should sustain the purity of the Church's awareness that its reality comes from God and goes to God. It can never reduce itself to earthly being and activity, however laudable they might be, without losing its identity and ceasing to exist.

> Under the impulse of love, which the Holy Spirit pours into their hearts (cf. Rom. 5:5), they live more and more for Christ and for his Body, the Church (cf. Col. 1:24). The more fervently, therefore, they join themselves to Christ by this gift of their whole life, the fuller does the Church's life become and the more vigorous and fruitful its apostolate.[14]

It is clear that the religious life does not relate to the structure of the Church in the same way as the hierarchy. It is not part of what is strictly required for a church as a condition of its existence. A church can't exist without priests who distribute the sacraments and the word, nor without people to receive them. But the hierarchy and Christian people constitute the minimal conditions. If we envision the Church in its fullness, in its completeness, then it necessarily requires lives entirely consecrated to God. The experience of the bishops attests that where the monastic life does not yet exist, one cannot say that the Church is entirely rooted.

> The state of life, then, which is constituted by the profession of the evangelical counsels, while not entering into the hierarchical structure of the Church, belongs undeniably to her life and holiness.[15]

2
Religious Life in the Church

The essential doctrine on profession is found mainly in the first and last numbers of chapter 10 of the Statutes.[1] They were inspired by Vatican Council II which, in the light of the doctrine on the Church developed in the decrees *Lumen Gentium* and *Perfectae Caritatis*, gave a magisterial teaching on the religious life.

THE THEOLOGY OF THE CHURCH ACCORDING TO VATICAN COUNCIL II

THE HISTORICAL CONTEXT

With earlier theologians (for instance, St Thomas), there was no separate treatise on the Church. Rather, it was a diffuse reality, present in each of the great mysteries of the faith, for example, the incarnation, redemption, etc. It was the difficulties raised in the controversies of the time of the Protestant Reformation which led to the development of a systematic theology. The idea of a community served as a basis for an intellectual synthesis, necessarily quite polemical and defensive, whose boundaries were to become evident with time. In consequence, alongside the notion of community, that of the 'Mystical Body' was introduced, without, however, arriving at a perfect integration of the two notions. The mystical and the concrete, the interior and exterior remained juxtaposed.

The radical commitment to unity, the sense of the laity whose active presence in the Church is affirmed, the notion of the Church as bearing light for all of humanity, greater knowledge of the Oriental Churches – all this influenced the constitution on the Church of Vatican Council II, the constitution in which the Church became aware of its own reality.

THE MYSTERY OF THE CHURCH

The Church arises from the Trinity. From its origins it bears the mark of the Three Persons with whom humanity is established in a union of being and love through baptism. It is the eternal plan of the Father that is realised in the Church. The Word incarnate is its instrument through his redemptive mission. The Spirit animates the Church which issued from his sacrifice. The Church by its nature strives towards the Kingdom of God by an earthly path that follows Christ. On earth it is the Church of the poor. It is at the same time visible and spiritual; it is only from its interior wellspring that we can understand its concrete and visible reality.

The Word of God opens multiple perspectives to us on this essential mystery, through the images that it uses to describe the Church: house, vine, flock, Spouse, mystical Body, heavenly Jerusalem . . .

THE PEOPLE OF GOD

One image is particularly underlined: the Church is the People of God; not a static entity, but a people who are journeying and being built up throughout the changes and chances of human history.

Each member of this people, each Christian, is a participant in the priesthood of Christ: this priesthood entitles them to participate actively and specifically in the worship given to the Father, by spreading the message of salvation, and by establishing in the secular world the reign of justice and Christian love.

The nature of the people of God is essentially catholic, that is to say, universal: God wants to save all people. Certain people benefit completely from all the gifts with which God has endowed his Church; this kernel must be the instrument of the realisation of the design of the Father for the world, and its sacrament or sign is the Catholic Church. Others make use of a more or less considerable part of its resources: baptism can incorporate them into Christ, and they can even enjoy an authentic hierarchy. This gives them a true participation, even though it is incomplete, in the life of the Church. We must consider as participating in some way, limited but real, in the life of the Church, even those who don't believe in Christ, but who have a religious life (especially the Jews), or, at the extreme limit, those who, without even believing in God, still have a soul open to his grace. All are family in Christ.

THE HIERARCHICAL ESTABLISHMENT OF THE CHURCH

To make sure that the people of God have pastors and the resources for growth, Christ instituted ministers in his Church who work for the good of the entire body. These are the successors of Peter and the apostles: the pope and the bishops, collegially united in their care for the Church, and priests and deacons, etc. The constitution produced valuable clarifications on the hierarchy in the Church, above all concerning the nature and the role of the episcopate, but this doesn't enter into our discussion here.

THE LAITY

The laity aren't merely non-clerics. To them is given their own vocation to 'seek the kingdom of God by engaging in temporal affairs and by ordering them according to the plan of God.'[2] Laity and clergy are a single people: the deep vocation, the fundamental dignity, the supreme destiny are identical for all.

UNIVERSAL CALL TO HOLINESS

The plan of God is to communicate himself to human beings by making of them one people who know him in truth and serve him in holiness.

Everything in the Church is at the service of this holiness of love to which all without exception – clergy, religious and laity – are called by Christ, following after him. 'Be perfect as your Father in heaven is perfect.' In every state of life, the perfection of charity can and should be realised. But we must use the necessary means.

But if charity is to grow and fructify in the soul like a good seed, each of the faithful must willingly hear the word of God and carry out his will with deeds, with the help of his grace; he must frequently partake of the sacraments, chiefly the Eucharist, and take part in the liturgy; he must constantly apply himself to prayer, self-denial, active brotherly service and the practice of all virtues. This is because love, as the bond of perfection and fullness of the law (cf. Col. 3:14; Rom. 13:10), governs, gives meaning to, and perfects all the means of sanctification. Hence the true disciple of Christ is marked by both love of God and his neighbour.

Therefore all the faithful are invited and obliged to holiness and the perfection of their own state of life. Accordingly let all of them see that they direct their affections rightly, lest they be hindered in their pursuit of perfect love by the use of worldly things and by an adherence to riches which is contrary to the spirit of evangelical poverty, following the apostle's advice: Let those who use this world not fix their abode in it, for the form of this world is passing away (cf. 1 Cor. 7:31, Greek text).[3]

MARTYRDOM

But certain of Christ's faithful are called to a more radical way. First, those who resemble the Master more closely, 'freely accepting death for the salvation of the world':

Since Jesus, the Son of God, showed his love by laying down his life for us, no one has greater love than he who lays down his life for him and for his brothers (cf. 1 Jn. 3:16; Jn. 15:13). Some Christians have been called from the beginning, and will always be called, to give this greatest testimony of love to all, especially to persecutors.[4]

THE COUNSELS

We know that tradition has seen life consecrated to God by the observance of the evangelical counsels as a pseudo-martyrdom, the same reality of love realised without the shedding of blood. After the martyrs, the constitution mentions those who have followed the evangelical counsels: first of all those who 'devote themselves to God alone more easily with an undivided heart (cf. 1 Cor. 7:32–4) in virginity or celibacy'; then those who imitate Christ, who ' "emptied himself, taking the form of a servant . . .and became obedient unto death" (Phil. 2:7–8) and for our sakes "became poor, though he was rich" (2 Cor. 8:9)'.

THE RELIGIOUS STATE

All Christians should follow the spirit of the counsels, according to the circumstances of their lives. However, religious have a specific vocation: for them, the counsels are the object of a public profession, a state of life recognised by the Church. Let us follow the text closely:

> The teaching and example of Christ provide the foundation for the evangelical counsels of chaste self-dedication to God, of poverty and of obedience. The Apostles and Fathers of the Church commend them, and so do her doctors and pastors. They therefore constitute a gift of God which the Church has received from her Lord and which by his grace she always safeguards.[5]

This divine gift, incarnate in the person and words of Christ, is entrusted first of all to the Church (which orders the practice of the counsels and oversees the forms of life based on them). Let us never forget that the call to follow Christ by the way of the counsels is always and primarily a gift to the Church, 'for the good of the entire Body of Christ', an ecclesial reality, even though intensely personal. This will have important consequences, as the one called ought to live from the life and the thought of the Church, ought to share its concerns and bear its intentions in prayer.

The Church thus has a care to order the practice of the counsels, to control the rules proposed by charismatic founders, to sustain established institutes. 'She herself receives, in the name of the authority which God has confided to her, the vow uttered by those who make profession.'

The varied families thus established are very profitable to the Church.

> Members of these families enjoy many helps towards holiness of life. They have a stable and more solidly based way of Christian life. They receive well-proven teaching on seeking after perfection. They are bound together in brotherly communion in the army of Christ. Their Christian freedom is fortified by obedience. Thus they are enabled to live securely and to maintain faithfully the religious life to which they have pledged themselves. Rejoicing in spirit they advance on the road of love.[6]

THE PROFESSION OF VOWS

How does one become a member of such a family? Through profession of vows. Let us look at the nature of these vows.

> The Christian who pledges himself to this kind of life binds himself to the practice of the three evangelical counsels by vows or other sacred ties of a similar nature. He consecrates himself wholly to God, his supreme love. In a new and special way he makes himself over to God, to serve and honour him.[7]

Here is expressed in the clearest possible way the meaning of the vows: the religious 'consecrates himself wholly to God' – why? For the love of God, 'his supreme love'. 'You will love the Lord your God with all your heart, with all your soul, and with all your mind.' The vows respond: 'Yes, Lord, here I am.'

It is a living person who consecrates himself to God. He gives himself with all his vitality, his capacities, physical, intellectual, affective, 'in a new and special way [he makes] himself over to God, to serve and honour him.'

A SECOND BAPTISM

Here we again converge with the first paragraphs of the Statutes. The consecration realised by religious profession does not begin from zero; it is grafted onto baptismal consecration.

In baptism we are incorporated into Christ by the gift of the Holy Spirit, who makes us adopted heirs of the Father, bearing in us a seed of divine and eternal life. We renounce Evil and all its works, we are radically purified from all sin, the Spirit makes us holy before God, and consecrates us to him.

Nothing in Christian dignity can surpass this fundamental sacrament. Baptism is the basis of everything. Profession is not a super-baptism giving birth to a super-Christian. It is rather the existential efflorescence of baptismal grace, assumed in an adult and free decision.

We can now appreciate the true value of the reason why the monastic tradition speaks of a second baptism when referring to profession. Expression and incarnation of the love of Christ, the most complete gift of self possible for a religious person, it obtains, in principle, remission of all previous sins and gives the religious rebirth in Christ, as an entirely new creature before God. In baptism, the sacrament effected this rebirth and this purification *ex opere operato*, by its own power, provided there was a living faith. Since profession isn't a sacrament, the purification is realised by the intensity of love of the one who vows himself to God. This effect should normally be total, because the vows objectively express a total love, but it must be admitted that it can be more or less so according to subjective dispositions. In any case, there is hardly any comparable opportunity for the adult Christian to make an act of such perfect and incarnate love.

3
Profession

The years in the novitiate lead to profession, when the novice covenants himself to the Lord through a public solemn promise, accepted by the Church. This promise, the vows he declares, effects the most radical gift of self a person can make, and constitutes the consecration of a person's whole being to God.

Profession gives the novice stability (for a set period or finally, according to circumstance) in the eternal movement of love (that is to say, in the Spirit) of the Son towards the Father. As the Word has taken flesh in the man, Jesus, the love of the professed incarnates itself in the freely assumed commitment to follow Jesus, poor, chaste, obedient, in this community, according to this rule of life. This implies perseverance in the refusal to become entrenched, open to All through what is closely delineated, in submission to the demand of love.

Jesus is the way, the truth, the life. He calls those whom he chooses to follow him more closely by way of the evangelical counsels: if you want to be perfect, sell everything and follow me. The practice of these counsels, evolved by the Church little by little in institutional form, is the means of arriving at the most perfect conformity to Christ and thus to Love.

You know the historical stages by which the religious state emerged:

— the apostles around Jesus, the community of disciples at Jerusalem (Acts);
— the consecrated celibate, first of all widows (1 Timothy

5:3–16), then virgins, living at home but already fulfilling the primordial function of religious: '[continuing in] supplications and prayers night and day' (1 Timothy 5:5);
— monks in the fourth century in Egypt and elsewhere, who retired into solitude (*eremos*, from which we derive eremitical life), individually or collectively (cenobitic life).

From the beginning a period of probation and formation before admission to the monastic state was required, but its duration varied quite considerably. It was finally set at one year. The end of this probation was marked by the more or less explicit commitment to practise the evangelical counsels, of which acceptance was signified by reception of the monastic habit. Formal vows were introduced later. Frequently only the vow of obedience was made, poverty and chastity being implicit in the obligations of monastic life.

Western monks have given more precise juridical contours to monastic life. St Benedict in the sixth century required vows of stability (the monk was to remain in the monastery – this was new), conversion of manners (consecrating the evangelical conversion that is at the heart of monastic life, and which has no limit or end), and obedience. In general, the monastic tradition in the West has adopted this formula – the Carthusians included, with a small change in the order of the vows (stability, obedience and conversion of manners), doubtless owing to the influence of the Order of St Ruf, from which two of the first Carthusians came.

In the Middle Ages, in the monastic Orders in general, solemn profession was made after one year of novitiate. And apparently most persevered! Then came the Reformation, the social and intellectual revolution of 1789, the rationalism and atheism of the masses of the nineteenth and twentieth centuries, the pluralism and materialism of our time. Access to the final religious commitment had to be prolonged in order to enable a deeper formation and a freer and more stable commitment.

With us:

in 1839 – 2 years of novitiate, then solemn profession;

in 1851 – 1 year of novitiate, 4 years of simple perpetual vows,[1] then solemn profession;

in 1924 – 1 year of novitiate, 4 years of temporary vows, solemn profession;

in 1949 – 2 years of novitiate, 3 years of temporary vows, solemn profession;

in 1969 – 2 years of novitiate, 5 years of temporary vows (3 with the novitiate, 2 with the solemnly professed), solemn profession.

These adjustments have been necessary, but haven't been very effective. Perseverance at the Grande Chartreuse in the seventeenth and eighteenth centuries was 94.6 per cent and 93.1 per cent respectively. In the nineteenth century it was 72 per cent, in the twentieth, until 1975, 55 per cent.

Departure totals: 45 per cent (33 per cent after first profession, 12 per cent after solemn profession).

The reasons? New attitudes in regard to commitments in general (divorce, for example), lack of human and spiritual maturity, preoccupation with human fulfilment, an unstable world, with evolving values, a different function of the novitiate and temporary vows (time of trying out, 'wait and see'?). The reasons are many and complex, this is certain.

In any case, the goal remains the same: solemn profession, definitive consecration of all our being to the Lord. The preliminary stages are necessary to clarify and set free our liberty, but even temporary vows are already animated with a desire for permanence and totality – if God wills it. Love has no other language.

4

Forgetfulness and Creation

In this conference I want to try not simply to communicate ideas to you but rather share an experience with you; better, a way of being that is central and important for me. I will use words and images but to evoke another level of reality which I invite you to enter. Let us therefore begin with a time of silence, because it is silence that will be our place of communion.

Put yourselves in a relaxed position, remaining alert. Close your eyes. Enter within yourself. Let your awareness inhabit your body; welcome the movement of your breathing; slow it down a bit. Be fully and peaceably there, from the centre of your being to its edge. You are. Let us be this way together in silence for a moment . . .

I am going to talk now. I ask you to listen to me at the level of your inmost being, with the ear of your silence. I will leave expanses of silence during the reading. Let what the words evoke live in your heart.

> I want to know Christ and the power of his resurrection and the sharing of his sufferings by becoming like him in his death, if somehow I may attain the resurrection from the dead. Not that I have already obtained this or have already reached the goal; but I press on to make it my own, because Christ Jesus has made me his own. Beloved, I do not consider that I have made it my own; but this one thing I do: forgetting what lies behind and straining forward to what lies ahead, I press on towards the goal

for the prize of the heavenly call of God in Christ Jesus. (Philippians 3:10–14)

'Forgetting what lies behind and straining forward to what lies ahead, I press on towards the goal.'

Profession, simple or solemn, cannot be a conclusion in an absolute sense. It is a conclusion in regard to the past; it is a point of departure in regard to the future. And Paul insists that we should strain forward to what lies ahead. The way travelled is to be forgotten: no vain remorse, no 'if only', no complacency on account of hoarded spiritual riches.

Before God we are always indifferent servants, pardoned sinners, poor ones. Let us not close our hands on nothing, but keep them open towards the Lord in order to receive the munificence of his love. We are his children in the measure that we are born of God; and it is naked that we are born.

The power to forget is very important. It allows us to get rid of resentments and marks of honour, defilements and exterior burdens from our past, so that we only keep what is inscribed on the substance of our being, by which we are that which we are in the present moment. Thus casting everything aside, we can run ahead, buoyant and responsive,[1] everything straining for the goal which lies ahead, in a perpetual going beyond everything already attained, never pausing in this life. 'Draw me after you, let us make haste' (Canticle 1:4). Christ is always ahead. Union with God presents itself as perpetual newness, a continual beginning to begin again. We climb the ladder that links earth and heaven, the one which Jacob saw; God calls us to come up to him. The ladder is Christ and every rung reached opens always towards something beyond. We find ourselves always beginning in regard to that which is beyond.

> For the person who runs towards the Lord, the wide space for his divine race will never be lacking. For he must always rise and never stop running towards the one

who says: 'Rise and come', each time giving the grace to rise higher.[2]

This continual going beyond self isn't a particular stage in the spiritual life, it is the very condition of our being. The spirit, an immaterial and intelligible reality, is, in itself, unlimited. In this, God and the soul are of one nature.

> But God is the uncreated reality and the creator of beings, who is always what he is . . .There is another aspect, the reality brought into existence through creation which is always turned towards the first cause and is sustained in the good by participation in the Reality which surrounds it, so much so that in a certain sense it is continually created, growing by its deepening in the good, in such a way that in it too no limit is to be seen, nor can its growth in the good, in love, be circumscribed by any boundary.[3]

The created being can always become greater. If God is infinite in action, the soul is infinite in becoming. Its divinity consists in being transformed into God. If it is infinite in becoming, its creation necessarily takes the form of growth, without which it would be merely finite, which characterises the material world. In this perspective, the continual progress is constitutive of the soul itself, it keeps it always turned towards something beyond itself.

There is something of prime importance here for our way of living day by day.

Let us try another little experience. Close your eyes, breathe two or three times, deeply and slowly. Become aware of your body, then enter into yourself to the source of your being. Then, sitting there, peacefully, visualise yourself on the screen of your imagination. See your body irradiated with light. It is thus that you are wrapped in the love of God, love that gives you being in your material existence – the breath that we receive expresses this well – and gives you your spiritual existence. Existence as a created spirit capable of unlimited growth in knowledge and love. Existence as adopted children of God who plunges us into his own intimate life. This life is communicated to us in each instant by a relationship of grace and liberty that permits us to grow endlessly in goodness and love even to the fullness of Christ which is without end.

Let us be aware of this light of love that surrounds us. Love touches us through each object that we see, great or small, the mountain and the tree, the sun and the candle-flame. It sings in the song of birds, beckons in the murmur of the brook. It takes a human face with Christ, but also in each of the brothers who rubs shoulders with us. It breaks into our life through all the events which form it. It is constant in our heart, a presence of the Lord whose name accents our breathing. We breathe the love who creates us, here and now.

Consciously, and with confident surrender, I open myself to this life and this light which, on God's side, are eternal; the creative action of God, in God, is God himself. Only its effects are in time. Each present moment links me with eternity, bears me as a child to the Father in the love of the Spirit. This moment is rich with the entire past, and bears in itself the future in the measure that I commit myself to it in faith. Forgetting the past, I press on wholeheartedly towards the goal, letting myself be borne by the flow of the present.

It is precisely the reality of my actual participation in the life of God which, overwhelming me, enflames my desire and turns it towards its wellspring. I turn by forgetting, by the poverty of my empty hands. I soar up on my desire. Each instant is an absolute beginning. I receive myself anew, and I give myself in all simplicity. The joy of my gratitude and my praise for the love and mercy of God that enfold me are the song of my creation.

But that which is obtained cannot become a limit to my desire. This is not God. The most dazzling light, the most intense feeling of love, the greatest revelation of his beauty, this is still not the One who is infinite, incomprehensible, always beyond. To be with him, I must thus go always further to encounter his newness without end.

To reach the Creator, I must myself become a creator – at least as regards the disposition of the spirit. I must smash all the moulds in which I continually shape myself, because they are always limited; I must reject all security, familiar words, riches, offer myself utterly poor, virgin, to the breath of the Spirit. Thus is our creativity made possible, the only creativity that counts, which forms Christ in us, which gives birth to the Son, the creativity which forms us, our selves; not just any created work, but our selves, in a poem of love to God, a poem that is absolutely unique.

Sometimes it is by solemn words of love that the Spirit gives me being, sometimes by joyous ones. There are very ordinary words, bread, water; there are words of humiliation, of suffering, even of sin. We must allow ourselves to be formed by these words so that the glory of God may be sung.

If I am the poet of the poem that is my life, I am also a priest. The Word that is given me – as a Christian[4] and, in eminent fashion, as a priest – has the power to change everything into the body of Christ. This is my body. This is my blood, poured out for you. As God creates, in each instant, through his Word, he thus recreates us, reassumes us in all our humanity, with all the creation, in an eternal offering of the love of Christ to the Father, into the heart of which the Mass plunges us.

Let us together live a day of creation. Let us enter into ourselves until we come to the level from which springs the source of our being. Each morning is an absolute beginning. God creates the heavens and the earth in this instant. I open my eyes on the morning of creation, I receive the gift of being, wholly new, from the hands of God. Our first movement should be a surge of wonder and gratitude. The sun rises. We should hasten to meet this love that comes to us in the tasks and happenings of our day, however little they are. Let us be attentive to the secret presence of love that enfolds us, to its tenderness, sometimes very personal. This inventive attention, this confidence and receptivity are, perhaps, a very simple form of continual prayer. Let us receive the words of our poem in joy and surrender to the Spirit who inspires them, whether or not they are pleasing to our ear. What do we know? When the words surpass our comprehension, when the melody is dissonant, unexpected, or full of half tones, we escape our limits, we go beyond. This melody, these words that are so simple, so concrete, are secretly infused with the Word, bear the form of Christ, say, 'Father'.

> In the beginning was the Word, and the Word was with God and the Word was God . . . All things came into being through him, and without him not one thing came into being. What has come into being in him was life, and the life was the light of all people. (John 1:1–4)

Each morning let us plunge our being, our day, into the torrent of love that floods from the Father to the Son by the Spirit, to rise again from the Son to the Father in the surge of Love. This is the creation, this is the Mass. Let us welcome, consecrate, offer ourselves, our strophe for today in the eternal eucharist, the thanksgiving to love. What is given no longer belongs to us; our offering is the passage (the passover) of our life in God. It goes through the dispossession of forgetting, in the single remembrance of God. We turn ourselves, we advance in faith and confidence towards the One who comes and who will come.

Each hour of the Office repeats this consecration and this praise. This prayer isn't a parenthesis in our life, but a special

time, because in each instant, in each thing, person, circumstance, God communicates himself, his Son becomes
incarnate, the Spirit unites in the invisible bonds of love.

'And God saw all that he had made, and indeed, it was
very good. And there was evening and there was morning'
(Genesis 1:31). In the evening, I give back my being to
the Father; I surrender life to him, and entrust myself in the
repose of the seventh day. Each night I die in faith, having
only my poverty, and my trust and peace in a hope that
wishes neither to count nor to know anything.

Isn't the Father here, the Father whose love catches sight
of me, even when I am far off? He runs and puts his arms
around my neck and covers me with kisses. 'But Father, I
have sinned!' 'Quick, bring the most beautiful robe . . . a ring
for his finger, sandals . . .'

Thus we proceed, flowers of a day, 'from beginnings, in
beginnings, through beginnings that never end.'[5]

Maranatha

5
Obedience in the Bible

The Word of God calls all creation into existence and it obeys with joy.

> The One who prepared the earth for all time . . .
> who sends forth the light and it goes;
> he called it, and it obeyed him, trembling;
> the stars shone in their watches, and were glad;
> he called them, and they said, 'Here we are!'
> They shone with gladness for him who made them.
>
> (Baruch 3:32–5)

Thus all creatures hasten to the voice of God and take their place in the cosmic harmony. The Lord has willed that one of his creatures be its priest, giving glory to his Creator by his consciousness and freedom, giving voice to mute beauty. Human beings refused to obey; in their pride, they wanted to be God.

Obedience is the submission of the person to the will of God, the fulfilment of a commandment whose value and meaning we can't always see. This obedience is the fruit of faith that clings to God for himself and submits to every word of God, thus entering into the pattern which he weaves in the history of the world. Faith and obedience coinhere.

ABRAHAM

To save the fallen world, God awakened the faith of Abraham and purified it in the crucible of obedience. 'Leave your country' (Genesis 12:1); 'Walk in my presence and be perfect' (Genesis 17:1); 'Take your son . . .and offer him as a holocaust' (Genesis 22:2). Abraham's entire existence rests on the Word: he moves constantly towards the Promise which constantly evades him and grows greater; he must do things which touch him to the quick, yet whose meaning escapes him. God tests Abraham; then he recognises in him an echo of his own heart: 'You have not withheld your son, your only son' (Genesis 22:16).

THE COVENANT

God chose a people to be his own and to serve his plan. He gave them a law to make them worthy of him. The people were to respond with faith and obedience. ' "All that the Lord has spoken we will do, and we will be obedient" ' (Exodus 24:7). This obedience is not the submission of a slave but an act of love. It is enough to review the *Shema*:

'Hear, O Israel: The Lord is our God, the Lord alone. You shall love the Lord your God with all your heart, and with all your soul, and with all your might. Keep these words that I am commanding you today in your heart. . . .You must diligently keep the commandments of the Lord your God, and his decrees, and his statutes that he has commanded you.'

(Deuteronomy 6:4–6,17)

The Psalms celebrate the law as the great gift of God to Israel and the source of loving obedience (Psalm 18:8–11 and all of Psalm 118). The pagans had natural law inscribed in their heart. But both, aspiring to this in the depth of the heart, in fact find themselves incapable of obeying the law of God. Wounded in their integrity, slaves of sin, Jew and pagan lock themselves in disobedience (Romans 3:10; 11:32). The prophets speak of a living law that will be written by the Spirit in the human heart, transforming it, giving it instinctive obedience from within; they announce a New Covenant (Jeremiah 31:33) in which all will be grace. They also obscurely catch a glimpse of the bowed down and humiliated figure who, through his innocent suffering, will redeem the disobedience of the people; a Servant in a state of continual obedience: 'Morning by morning he wakens – wakens my ear' (Isaiah 50:4).

CHRIST

In Jesus, the key to the human drama is given us. His obedience exceeds the wide limits of all human history, and even of creation, to root itself in the eternal and mysterious act by which, in the intimacy of God, the Father says his unique Word in pure light and, in return, receives this Word in pure Love (cf. Isaiah 55:11).

JESUS

Everything in Jesus is directed to the will of God; to do this is his food and his life. In consequence, he shows himself obedient to all that incarnates this will: Jewish law, his parents, the authorities – but freely. Our Statutes, and the Council, set Jesus' obedience before us as an example. Let us try to understand this in his historical life, which will give us a rather nuanced picture.

IN THE SYNOPTICS

Jesus was not an infant prodigy. Everything that we know of his youth is contained in Luke's brief statement: 'The child grew and became strong, filled with wisdom; and the favour of God was upon him' (Luke 2:40).

The first of his words that the evangelists report were addressed to his parents when they returned, seeking him in the temple at Jerusalem where he was debating with the doctors of the law. Jesus was twelve years old, the age of religious maturity in Judaism; he showed a clear awareness of his personal identity.

> 'Child, why have you treated us like this? Look, your father and I have been searching for you in great anxiety.' He said to them, 'Why were you searching for me? Did you not know that I must be in my father's house?' (Luke 2:48–9)

Everything is here in potential: his filial awareness, his absolute consecration to the work of his heavenly Father, the subordination of every human tie to it. But this is only one episode. His hour has not yet come. Jesus goes down to Nazareth with Joseph and Mary. The ordinary life of the little family of the humble carpenter of Nazareth, his wife and his child, resume its daily round. We can imagine many things about this life which lasted for thirty of the thirty-three years of the life of Jesus; we know nothing. The Gospel is satisfied with saying, 'He was obedient to them.' Obedience, no longer of an infant, but the free obedience of an adolescent and then a man, aware of his personality and his liberty; submission to Joseph who represented to him his heavenly Father. Thus 'Jesus increased in wisdom and in years, and in divine and human favour' (Luke 2:52).

Let us note the absence of adolescent rebellion. Jesus affirms himself in peace and with continuity. There is no question of higher education, sexual experiences, foreign travel, social or economic responsibility, or any of the things that we have a tendency to deem necessary today to become an adult. In the simple and humble life that was his, in the limited context and poverty of a small village, with periodic pilgrimages to Jerusalem, a perfect man is formed under the eye of his Father.

His public life opens with the baptism he receives from John. The note of obedience is found in the enigmatic words of Jesus: ' "Let it be so now; for it is proper for us in this way to fulfil all righteousness" ' (Matthew 3:15), that is to say to submit together to God's plan. Then, 'led by the Spirit' (Luke 4:1), Jesus goes to the desert to be tested; his entire life will be led by the Spirit of God.

His redemptive mission is conceived as an obedience to the Father, as a living out of a divine disposition, following the role of the Suffering Servant prefigured in Isaiah. Jesus declares himself servant of all: ' "For the Son of Man came not to be served but to serve and to give his life a ransom for many" ' (Mark 10:45). The divine plan is 'just' and concerns the last days; he simply accomplishes it. ' "Yet not my will but yours be done" ' (Matthew 26:42; Luke 22:42).

But he wasn't a 'visionary' in the pejorative sense. He obeyed the will of God transmitted through the Bible, through those who exercised legitimate authority, religious or political, through Jewish institutions (for example, the payment of the Temple tax – Matthew 17:24–7), in general through the events which he read as the signs of the times. He went as far as handing himself over without resisting to the human powers who acted unjustly.

'Do not think that I have come to abolish the law or the prophets; I have come not to abolish but to fulfil.' (Matthew 5:17)

He taught his disciples to pray to the Father each day: 'Your

will be done on earth as it is in heaven.' In doing the will of
God, we are in communion with God, we are his children,
and brothers and sisters among ourselves.

'Here are my mother and my brothers! Whoever does the
will of God is my brother and sister and mother.' (Mark
3:34–5)

An extraordinary saying: human ties are surpassed by the
bonds born of love and obedience to God.

In what way did he know the will of the Father so that he
could do it? There is, first of all, the mysterious communion
between the Father and the Son.

'I thank you, Father, Lord of heaven and earth, because
you have hidden these things from the wise and the intel-
ligent and have revealed them to infants; yes, Father, for
such was your gracious will. All things have been handed
over to me by my Father, and no one knows the Son
except the Father, and no one knows the Father except
the Son and anyone to whom the Son chooses to reveal
him.' (Matthew 11:25–7)

And there is the interior light of the Spirit. This light clarifies
the created means through which God communicates his
will to us, the signs which speak of it: first of all, the Word
of God of which Jesus shows an intimate knowledge, and
where he finds the foreshadowing and meaning of his
mission. Then his parents to whom he is obedient, the legitimate political and religious authorities to which he hands
himself over without resisting, even when they act unjustly.
He sees these as instruments of the Father's plan.

His attitude in regard to Jewish law is nuanced. In general,
he submits to it. As a pious Jew he wears a fringe on his
cloak (Matthew 9:20), observes feasts, shows himself full of
zeal for the temple (Mark 11:15–18), frequents the syna-
gogues on the Sabbath, and assumes the role of rabbi.

At the same time, he is very critical in regard to the legalistic and excessively exacting tendencies of a certain piety which split hairs over the Mosaic law in the name of Jewish tradition ('the tradition of men'), which he refuses to put on the same level as the law of Moses – as did the Jewish religion of his time (Matthew 23:1–36).[1] He shows a certain liberty in his relation to its usages and excuses his disciples when faced with the Pharisees (Matthew 12:1–8). Jesus recalls the hierarchy of the precepts, the primacy of the law of love. He is not a troublemaker on principle, but there are cases where it is impossible to avoid confrontation: the questions of the Sabbath, and the rites of purity, for example. He scandalises by healing on the Sabbath (Matthew 12:9–14). He pronounces what, for the Pharisees, is a sacrilege:

> 'The sabbath was made for humankind, and not humankind for the sabbath; so the Son of Man is lord even of the sabbath.' (Mark 2:27)

As for the rules of exterior religious purity, Jesus refuses to submit to them when they force him to discriminate in his relationships and not associate with sinners (Mark 2:17), which would contradict the good news of pardon which he has come to proclaim.

For Jesus is aware of being sent by his Father to reveal the pure and absolute will of God and thus fulfil the law, that is to say, to bring it to its perfection. ' "Do not think that I have come to abolish the law or the prophets; I have come not to abolish but to fulfil" ' (Matthew 5:17). He bears 'a new teaching with authority' (Mark 1:27), not, to be sure, in contradiction to the revelation of God in the Mosaic law, but, on certain points, making it more demanding and in greater conformity to the primordial intention of God (Matthew 5:17–48; 19:8–9).

' "You have heard what was said by our forefathers . . .But

I tell you . . ." ' Jesus puts himself above Moses and declares, by his own authority as the Son, the will of God. It is not simply a question of better moral teaching, but of the Person of Christ and the event of his life, death, and resurrection. The passage from the Old Testament to the New is effected by a new action of God within the reality of history. The gift of God that was the law is assumed and given anew in the divine and gratuitous pardon that Christ realises in his person and that he proclaims. We move from the rule of the law to that of grace and faith in Christ. It is the folly of the love of God that establishes the Christian moral requirement, which aspires to the response of love without limit. The gift of God isn't a reward for the observance of a law, however laudable that is. On the contrary, the gift of love, the gift of the Spirit, received by faith, makes possible and demands a life of love. It is not a question of replacing one exterior law by another, even if it might be a better one. The law of the New Covenant is Christ, inscribed by the Holy Spirit in the heart that he transforms in his image.

Therefore, in reality, Jesus finds himself in an attitude of conflict in regard to the law and religious authorities. His absolute obedience to God and his fidelity to his mission entail a certain conflict with an authority, itself of divine origin. But Jesus sees this in his Father's plan, and submits, fully realising 'the most intimate essence and the deepest tendency of the Old Testament', of the law which, however, condemns him to die.[2]

It is a man who dies on the cross, and his sensibility recoils before this atrocious destiny.

> 'My Father, if it is possible, let this cup pass from me; yet not what I want but what you want.' (Matthew 26:39)

This is human obedience. ' "The spirit indeed is willing, but the flesh is weak" ' (v. 41). The Father responds by resurrecting the weak flesh, and giving it his glory.

OUR OBEDIENCE

Jesus also requires obedience of his disciple:

> 'Everyone then who hears these words of mine and acts on them will be like a wise man who built his house on rock.' (Matthew 7:24)

Not an obedience of the lips, but of acts:

> 'Not everyone who says to me, "Lord, Lord," will enter the kingdom of heaven, but only the one who does the will of my Father who is in heaven.' (Matthew 7:21)

And what does he say of the two sons?

> 'A man had two sons; he went to the first and said, "Son, go and work in the vineyard today." He answered, "I will not"; but later he changed his mind and went. The father went to the second and said the same; and he answered, "I go, sir"; but he did not go. Which of the two did the will of his father?' (Matthew 21:28–30)

The mission of the Church is to teach us obedience to Christ.

> 'All authority in heaven and on earth has been given to me. Go therefore and make disciples of all nations, baptising them in the name of the Father and of the Son and of the Holy Spirit, and teaching them to obey everything that I have commanded you.' (Matthew 28:18–20)

NOTE

One can speak of the 'disobedience' of Jesus in regard to the authorities of the Synagogue of his time. Christ is therefore also a model for those who decided that it is better to obey God rather than men (Acts 5:29); which signifies, let us note well, that the motive for their attitude is not a claiming of autonomy and the right to independence, but obedience to God. Jesus was ready to obey the ecclesiastical authority of his times, in spite of the personal unworthiness of those who were its representatives (' "The scribes and the Pharisees sit on Moses' seat; therefore, do whatever they teach you and follow it; but do not do as they do for they do not practice what they teach" ', Matthew 23:2–3). The freedom which he is aware of in his nature as Son does not stop him from paying the Temple tax, in order not to scandalise the officials who claimed it from him (Matthew 17:24–7). Nonetheless, in spite of this obedience, it is in the conflict with the religious authority of the people of the Covenant, his own people, that the life of Jesus reaches its culmination; and Jesus himself sees in this conflict the decreed will of the Father, recorded in advance in the holy books of this people (Matthew 21:33–45; 26:5–56; Mark 12: 1–12; Luke 20:9–19; 22:37). This is to say that Jesus' obedience to his Father finds itself in a situation willed by God, where he had to enter into a conflict of 'disobedience' in regard to another authority which, in its essence, also emanates from a divine disposition.

But this 'disobedience' of Christ has another aspect: in its inspiration and its motivations, it has nothing to do with the moral sentiment of a man who lays claim in an individualistic way to the right to be his own master, not even with a conscience that takes itself for the voice of God. From this fact, his 'disobedience' itself implies the recognition of God's authority in the human and institutional form which the transmission of his will has taken on. One might say that this 'disobedience', far from being a rebellion of a free subject who, aware of his autonomy, only reclaims his explicit right, was an obedience in the perfect sense of the word and under all the aspects which constitute an obedience of the type which we have just described.

So it is no longer difficult to understand why the theology of the primitive Christian community, when it approaches the theme of the conflict of Jesus with the Synagogue, takes delight in underlining not so much the superiority that his nature as Son of God conferred on him in relation to the Law, but the fact that Jesus, precisely thanks to his disobedience, realises in its fullness the inmost essence and most profound tendency of the Old Testament, as one sees them expressed in the Law and the Prophets.

This being said, it must not pass unnoticed that Jesus can be the model of a disobedience which, especially today, cannot be excluded as a possibility, indeed sometimes an obligation, vis-à-vis an ecclesiastical authority.

Karl Rahner, *Serviteurs du Christ* (Mame, 1969), p. 154

6

Obedience in St John

THE OBEDIENCE OF JESUS

John's contemplative gaze exposes profound realities. Jesus is the Word, the only Son of God, equal with God (5:18) and God himself (1:1). Thanks to the mystery of the incarnation, the dependency within equality of the Son in relationship to the Father in the heart of the Blessed Trinity is, as it were, itself translated into human form by a complete and humble voluntary submission.

Jesus comes into the world charged with a mission in the name of the Father, 'not to do my own will but the will of him who sent me' (5:30; 6:38). He often refers to his Father as 'the One who sent me', thus assuming the position of the one who is sent by a command to complete the work of God (4:34). All of Jesus' life, all his activity, hangs on the will of the Father.

> 'Very truly I tell you, the Son can do nothing on his own, but only what he sees the Father doing; for whatever the Father does, the Son does likewise.' (5:19)

> 'I can do nothing on my own. As I hear, I judge; and my judgement is just, because I seek to do not my own will but the will of him who sent me.' (5:30)

That which he *sees* the Father doing, what he *hears*; the source of Jesus' word and activity is in the contemplation of the Father; his gaze never leaves him, his ear is always attuned to him. He makes the Father's will his own in a continual and completely responsive receptivity.[1] His words are uncompromising.

'I always do what is pleasing to him.' (8:29)

'My food is to do the will of him who sent me and to complete his work.' (4:34)

The Jews betrayed Jesus, the Romans crucified him, and in this Jesus saw the fulfilment of the Father's plan. Flogged, bound, an object of mockery, he could serenely declare to Pilate: ' "You would have no power over me unless it had been given you from above" ' (19:11).

Jesus obeyed God alone; his submission was to the Father, beyond every human intermediary, in sovereign freedom.

'For this reason the Father loves me, because I lay down my life in order to take it up again. No one takes it from me, but I lay it down of my own accord. I have power to lay it down, and I have power to take it up again. I have received this command from my Father.' (10:17–18)

'Am I not to drink the cup that the Father has given me?' (18:11)

Why this radical submission? . . .Jesus' obedience is the concrete and irrefutable expression of his love: ' "I do as the Father has commanded me, so that the world may know that I love the Father" ' (14:31). Love, without constraint, spontaneously becomes conformed to the will of the beloved in an intimate union of hearts: ' "I have kept my Father's commandments and abide in his love" ' (15:10). This real and concrete action ensures the real and concrete presence of the Father: ' "And the one who sent me is with me; he has not left me alone, for I always do what is pleasing to him" ' (8:29).

This isn't always easy, because the work of the Father, the

salvation of humanity, leads him to the hour determined by the Father, 'his hour', at Calvary. ' "Now my soul is troubled. And what should I say – 'Father, save me from this hour?' No, it is for this reason that I have come to this hour. Father, glorify your name" ' (12:27–8). Jesus' obedience flows from his love for the Father and, in perfect disinterest, looks only to his glory. Jesus is unself-centred, and is not preoccupied with his own interests: ' "Yet I do not seek my own glory; there is one who seeks it and he is the judge" ' (8:50). The Father loves humanity, and wills its salvation. This love incarnates itself in Jesus, who gives himself totally to this work: ' "for their sakes I sanctify myself, so that they also may be sanctified in truth . . .so that the love with which you have loved me may be in them, and I in them" ' (17:19 and 26).

CHRISTIAN OBEDIENCE

The Word is made flesh, the Son gives himself over to death, in order that the love of God can be given to us in the Spirit. Becoming adopted heirs of God, we have to learn filial behaviour by watching and following the example of Jesus. The ideal would be that, in imitating Jesus, we could not do anything without gazing on our Father, and that, after Jesus' example, we would never seek our own egotistical interests, but only those of the Father.

Now by this we may be sure that we know him, if we obey his commandments. Whoever says, 'I have come to know him', but does not obey his commandments, is a liar, and in such a person the truth does not exist; but whoever obeys his word, truly in this person the love of God has reached perfection. By this we may be sure that

> we are in him: whoever says, 'I abide in him', ought to walk just as he walked. (1 John 2:3–6)

The foundation of our new life is an act of faith that isn't a simple adherence to abstract truth, but a personal encounter with Jesus, the divine Truth incarnate. In St John, to believe in Jesus is to accept him, to come to him, to listen to him, to follow him, to live in him. Hence, Christian life can consist only in imitating the behaviour of Christ, and above all, in plunging ourselves in the immense flow of his love for his Father, translated concretely and constantly into conformity to his will in everything.

> And this is his commandment, that we should believe in the name of his Son Jesus Christ and love one another, just as he has commanded us. All who obey his commandments abide in him, and he abides in them. And by this we know that he abides in us, by the Spirit that he has given us. (1 John 3:23–4)

It is now Jesus who reveals the will of the Father to us. The law of the new covenant is the person and the word of Jesus; it is the reverberation of the discovery of the love of God manifest in Christ, the joyous recognition, the way of acting of the children of God, the free and attentive conformity to the good pleasure of the Father.

'Jesus is the way, the truth and the life' (John 14:16). The way, in that he is the mediator of salvation. The Lord shares divine life with the one who believes in him. He goes before us on the way to the Father's house. The way, in that he incarnates the law or the will of God in himself, and becomes a rule of conduct for us. The term 'way' in the Old Testament frequently designates the Mosaic law (Psalm 119:1; Deuteronomy 5:33–6:1 etc.), the Gospel of John affirms in Jesus the fulfilment of the law and its positive values, and the substitution of Christ for the law: 'The law indeed was given through Moses; grace and truth came through Jesus Christ. No one has ever seen God. It is God the only Son, who is close to the Father's heart, who has made him known' (1:17–18). Jesus assumes the functions of the law: to reveal the face and the plan of the Father, to lead to life (5:24; 11:25). He is endowed with the divine attributes attached to the law in the Old Testament: Word of God, incarnate Wisdom, pre-existence with God, turned towards God, presence of God, the radiance of divine glory (1:1–14). John relates to Jesus the symbols denoting the law in Judaism: water of life, light, bread, wine. In short, John proclaims as outdated the economy of the old law and substitutes the person of Jesus for it. A living person succeeds the written law, the incarnate Word.

The words of Jesus are spirit and life (6:63). Whoever believes in him even though they die, will live (11:25). Life eternal is to know the Father, ' "the only true God, and Jesus Christ whom you have sent" ' (17:3).

For John, everything comes from the Father, but through the Son, and human beings can only return to the Father through the Christ. The Father loves the Son; the Son loves us as he is loved by the Father; we respond to divine love by loving the Master and our brothers and sisters. This love is demonstrated by our obedience.

> 'They who have my commandments and keep them are those who love me.' (14:21)

> 'As the Father has loved me, so I have loved you; abide in my love. If you keep my commandments, you will abide in my love, just as I have kept my Father's commandments and abide in his love.' (15:9–10)

This obedience enables us to enter the intimacy of the Lord in a relationship of reciprocal friendship. ' "You are my friends if you do what I command you" ' (15:14).

As friends of the Lord, we are brought into the intimacy of the Father, the Love who unites them sets us on fire in our turn: ' "Those who love me will keep my word, and my Father will love them, and we will come to them and make our home with them" ' (14:23). The Father and the Son in us can only communicate their Spirit to us; they transfigure us into the image of their love. A light can only illuminate; a fire can only enflame.

In this is love, not that we loved God but that he loved us and sent his Son to be the atoning sacrifice for our sins. Beloved, since God loved us so much, we ought also to love one another. No one has ever seen God; if we love one another, God lives in us, and his love is perfected in us. (1 John 4:10–12)

By this we know that we love the children of God, when we love God and obey his commandments. For the love of God is this, that we obey his commandments. And his commandments are not burdensome, for whatever is born of God conquers the world. And this is the victory that conquers the world, our faith. Who is it that conquers the world but the one who believes that Jesus is the Son of God?

(1 John 5:2–5)

7

Obedience in St Paul and in the Letter to the Hebrews

OBEDIENCE IN ST PAUL

For St Paul, the whole drama of the history of salvation comes down to a question of obedience to God.

> For just as one man's trespass led to condemnation for all, so one man's act of righteousness leads to justification and life for all. For just as by the one man's disobedience the many were made sinners, so by the one man's obedience the many will be made righteous. (Romans 5:19)

This obedience of Christ is inscribed in the creation of the world from its foundation.

> . . .he has made known to us the mystery of his will, according to his good pleasure that he set forth in Christ, as a plan for the fullness of time, to gather up all things in him, things in heaven and things on earth. (Ephesians 1:9–10)

The total, mutual gift of the divine Persons in the trinitarian life of love establishes a primary form of kenosis that is realised in the creation, above all in the free person. The Creator surrenders some of his freedom to him, but cannot in the end risk this adventure except by virtue of anticipation and acceptance of the second kenosis, and properly speaking, that of the cross, in which the Creator goes beyond the most extreme consequences of the disobedience of created freedom. There kenosis, as abandon of the form of God, becomes the distinctive act of love of the Son which translates his generation from and dependence on the Father into the expressive form of created obedience. The entire Trinity is engaged in this act: the Father being the one who sends the Son and abandons him on the cross, the Spirit who now only unifies the Father and the Son under the form of separation.

> [Christ] emptied himself,
>   taking the form of a slave . . .
>   he humbled himself and became obedient to the point
>   of death –
>   even death on a cross.
> Therefore God also highly exalted him
>   and gave him the name that is above every name . . .
>   (Philippians 2:7–9)

This, God's new intervention in history, effects a radical change in the relationship between God and human beings. It is a new economy of salvation and a new covenant. It is no longer through the observance of a law (Mosaic or natural) that human beings can be justified before God (a project that always ends in failure – Romans 2 and 3); but God gratuitously communicates his own justice in the gift of the Spirit to all, Jews or pagans, who believe in Christ.

> But now, irrespective of law, the righteousness of God has been disclosed, and is attested by the law and the prophets, the righteousness of God through faith in Jesus Christ for all who believe. For there is no distinction, since all have sinned and fall short of the glory of God; they are now justified by his grace as a gift, through the redemption that is in Christ Jesus . . .For we hold that a person is justified by faith apart from works prescribed by the law. (Romans 3:21–4, 28)

St Paul describes faith as an act of obedience, 'the obedience of faith' (Romans 16:26): obedience to the revelation of the grace of God in Jesus Christ is the fundamental act of our faith. This faith is pure grace that doesn't depend on any previous merit, but it is not fruitless: it fulfils what the law could not fulfil; the works of faith are not secondary, but second. 'Circumcision is nothing, and uncircumcision is nothing; but obeying the commandments of God is everything' (1 Corinthians 7:19).

God doesn't contradict himself. The requirement of the law (in essence, love of God and neighbour) will be fulfilled, but as a fruit of the gift of the Spirit, from within, freely. Christians are supremely free of all exterior constraints, not that they are able to do anything at all, but because they are given an interior source of life and love that makes them capable of spontaneously doing what the holy will of God wishes, which corresponds to the behaviour of the children of God, in the likeness of Christ.

The notion of law – and therefore of obedience – is not abolished, it is radically interiorised. The demand of love expresses itself through the 'law of the Spirit' (Romans 8:2), of the Spirit of Christ in our hearts. For Paul, as for John, the law is Christ: 'To those outside the law I became as one outside the law (though I am not free from God's law but am under Christ's law) so that I might win those outside the law' (1 Corinthians 9:21). There is a sort of dialectic between freedom and law. It becomes clear if we recall that the essence of freedom is to be able, of ourselves, to do good. We exercise this liberty when we act according to the truth of our being and of the being of things, inscribed in them by the Creator. The Spirit frees us in enabling our will to conform to the will of God, under the impulse of the love that he pours out in our heart. Thus obedience and liberty coincide.

. . .where the Spirit of the Lord is, there is freedom. (2 Corinthians 3:17)

> For freedom Christ has set us free . . . For in Christ Jesus . . . the only thing that counts is faith working through love. (Galatians 5:1, 6)

For greater clarity let us distinguish between interior freedom and exterior freedom: that is to say, the fact of not being constrained exteriorly by anyone else, by social, political, economic factors, etc.

Obviously Paul occupies himself little with this latter freedom. The Lord is near, we wait for his return, the appearances of this world pass away. Therefore remain in the state in which grace finds you, married or no, obey legitimate human and ecclesial authorities, parents, spouses, masters (Colossians 3:18–22), government authorities, seeing God's authority in them (Romans 13:10–11).

True life is the life of Christ in us, true freedom is the inner freedom of a child of God.

> . . . you have stripped off the old self with its practices and have clothed yourselves with the new self, which is being renewed in knowledge according to the image of its creator. In that renewal there is no longer Greek and Jew, circumcised and uncircumcised, barbarian, Scythian, slave and free; but Christ is all and in all! (Colossians 3:10–11)

Paul quietly affirms, 'you have stripped off the old self . . . and have clothed yourselves with the new self'. And this is true; in principle, baptism effects this. But Paul knows very well that interior liberty is not automatically restored: 'For I do not do the good I want, but the evil I do not want is what I do' (Romans 7:19). Effectually to want the good is frequently beyond our reach. We are not perfectly free to love in truth.

The gift of freedom, of the Spirit, is given to weak and wounded sinful people: 'But we have this treasure in clay jars, so that it may be made clear that this extraordinary power belongs to God and does not come from us' (2 Corinthians 4:7). We do not receive freedom ready made; God respects the laws of human growth. It is a seed of freedom that is planted in us, among the thorns of our wretchedness – a seed to be protected, cultivated, to which we must give the right living conditions, and from which we must remove obstacles that come from the old self that remains alive and well. In this perspective we rediscover the usefulness of exterior law, that of society and of the Church, that of religious profession based on the evangelical counsels; this law affords us support and education for our fragile and threatened freedom.

This enables us to see monastic obedience from Paul's perspective. He doesn't speak of it directly; it is a subsequent development over time. But by putting Christ's obedience in full light, as the centre of the work of salvation, and by inviting Christians to clothe themselves with the same mind ('let this mind be in you that was in Christ Jesus', Philippians 2:5), Paul establishes the foundation of religious obedience. The one whom the Lord calls to a more intimate participation with him in his work of salvation can only follow him in his kenosis.

Paul's preoccupation with the Mosaic law and the polemic of his times gives us a lesson that remains very pertinent. Our life is minutely ordered by a discipline, a positive 'law'. A legalism that robbed faith of its keenness, and blunted the primacy of freedom and charity would be a temptation for us.

We need rules of observance to educate and sustain our search for God. Besides, community life is not possible without a common law. The role of obedience is to free us from what is egotistical, illusory, short-sighted, 'fleshly' in us; to make us docile to the movement of the Holy Spirit; to make us transparent to the love that empties itself in giving itself. To fulfil this, we must obey as free persons, not to the letter, but consciously aspiring to the meaning incarnated in the letter[1] and 'interiorised' by us. Let us never forget that everything should be in the service of love, and that the conforming of our will to the Lord's, expressed in his Body, the Church, through the mediation of our superiors, is an exchange of intimacy, a bond of union with Christ, the most unfailing bond of all. Because, in the final analysis, it is to the Lord that our obedience is always given, not to human beings. The presence of Christ through his Spirit in the Church guarantees that those who hold authority authentically transmit the will of God to us. We will return to this point in the light of tradition.

OBEDIENCE IN THE LETTER TO THE HEBREWS

The letter to the Hebrews seems to address itself to a Judeo-Christian community, and is the only writing in the New Testament that gives Christ priestly titles. Christ is a high priest, compassionate, merciful and faithful;[2] his sacrifice is the fulfilment of the religion of the Old Testament and seals a new covenant. The life of Christ consists in a single movement from his coming into the world to his being raised to the right hand of the Father in heaven.

> For it is impossible for the blood of bulls and goats to take away sins. [So the religion of the Old Testament was ineffective.] Consequently, when Christ came into the world, he said,
>> 'Sacrifices and offerings you have not desired,
>> but a body you have prepared for me;
>> in burnt offerings and sin offerings
>> you have taken no pleasure.
>> Then I said, "See, God, I have
>> come to do your will, O God." ' (10:4–7)

> And it is by God's will that we have been sanctified through the offering of the body of Jesus Christ once for all. (10:10)

The entire unfolding of the life of Jesus is the expression of this fundamental obedience to the Father's plan of salvation. His sacrifice is not an isolated act of worship, it is his life, his death, consumed by the sacred fire of obedience and pleasing to the Father. Priest and sacrifice. But human.

> In the days of his flesh, Jesus offered up prayers and supplications, with loud cries and tears, to the one who was able to save him from death, and he was heard because of his reverent submission. Although he was a Son, he learned obedience through what he suffered; and having been made perfect, he became the source of eternal salvation for all who obey him, having been designated by God a high priest according to the order of Melchizedek. (5:7–10)

Christ took our sinners' death (which did not lead to God), freely assumed it, through a pure movement of love for us, in perfect union with the love that comes from the Father, and by this act, transformed it into a sacrifice (which leads to God). This sacrifice results in the transfiguration of the one who made the offering: Christ has been made perfect by his obedience and his sufferings. His body, utterly infused with divine life, resurrected, allows him to enter the true sanctuary 'not made with human hands' (see 9:11–12:24).

> For Christ did not enter a sanctuary made by human hands, a mere copy of the true one, but he entered into heaven itself, now to appear in the presence of God on our behalf. (9:24)

Christ is priest for eternity. He always intercedes for us before the Father.

> Therefore, my friends . . .we have confidence to enter the
> sanctuary by the blood of Jesus, by the new and living
> way that he opened for us through the curtain (that is
> through his flesh). (10:19–20)

Jesus has marked out for us a way of sacrifice and obedience
in hope and faith. Let us follow him with courage.

> Therefore, since we are surrounded by so great a cloud
> of witnesses, let us also lay aside every weight and the
> sin that clings so closely, and let us run with perseverance
> the race that is set before us, looking to Jesus the pioneer
> and perfecter of our faith, who for the sake of the joy
> that was set before him endured the cross, disregarding
> its shame, and has taken his seat at the right hand of the
> throne of God. (12:1–2)

This rich doctrine can help us to deepen the priestly sense
of our life as monks: the will to a complete obedience to
God, following Christ, the sufferings of life and death consecrated as sacrifice through obedience, interior transfiguration
that enables us to enter with Christ into the sanctuary of
God, intercession for our brothers and sisters before God,
perseverance in faith and hope. For us too it is our entire
life that should be our sacrifice.

Our religious consecration is priestly. In this sense, a
brother or a nun lives in its fullness the participation in
Christ's priesthood given in baptism.[3]

We should again note that it is a question of the obedience
of Jesus to God, not to human beings. At the end of the
letter there is an exhortation that sees obedience within
the Christian community as a duty of charity.

> Remember your leaders, those who spoke the word of
> God to you; consider the outcome of their way of life,
> and imitate their faith. . . .Obey your leaders and submit
> to them, for they are keeping watch over your souls and

will give an account. Let them do this with joy and not with sighing – for that would be harmful to you. (13:7 and 17)

8

Obedience in the Desert Fathers

We have seen that Christ's work of salvation is a work of obedience to God. Through it, the disobedience of humanity is redeemed, and those who believe in Christ are made capable of returning to the Father through love and conformity to his will.

Christ, for his part, calls his disciples to follow the road of freedom of renouncing self:

'Whoever comes to me and does not hate[1] father and mother, wife and children, brothers and sisters, yes, and even life itself, cannot be my disciple.' (Luke 14:26–7)

'If any want to become my followers, let them deny themselves and take up their cross and follow me.' (Matthew 16:24)

The first monks wanted to respond to this call, addressed to every disciple of Christ, in the most radical way possible. The account of Anthony's vocation clearly shows this. The renunciation should encompass not only that which we have but our very selves (Matthew 16:24). The practice of religious obedience was instituted to realise this: obedience to a human person and a rule of life. Thus religious obedience is only Christian obedience driven as far as it can go. It is the free and voluntary act of generosity of someone who wants to follow Christ without stopping on the way, who wants to give everything without reserve. Let us see how this evolution came about historically.

THE DESERT FATHERS

The immediate objective of the first Fathers' flight to the desert was to follow Christ in renunciation, the condition for the single-hearted search for God in solitude, a seeking that represented the ideal of the monk. The monk renounces Satan and the world to be faithful to Christ. This radical belonging to Christ had already given rise to the consecration of virgins and widows in the early days of Christianity.[2] The positive ideal of union with Christ dominated the asceticism of solitaries vowed to contemplation. They were convinced that contemplation of God is conditioned by purity of heart, to which the flesh, by reason of its state, after sin, constituted the principal obstacle. In the desert they engaged in fierce and pitiless combat through solitude, fasting, vigils, prayer and various practices of mortification.

Religious obedience was not initially practised. It is clear that the first great ascetics of the deserts did not practise it, since neither Anthony nor the other anchorites who began by retiring into absolute solitude obeyed any human being. Monastic obedience was discovered little by little, in the light of experience, as a very exalted spiritual good.

The elders knew very well how to discern the important from the less important in a life entirely organised with a view to union with God, but not everyone had this clarity. There was too much athletic asceticism, vain imitation and puerile competition that ended in catastrophes. Cassian tells the story of poor Benjamin who didn't want to conform either to the common custom in eating, or to submit himself to the elders' judgement. Instead of eating his two small pieces of bread each day, he obstinately insisted on taking them only every two days. Rebelling against all the advice of the elders, he became apostate and met a deplorable end.[3]

Examples of this sort opened their eyes to monastic prudence. They understood that the renunciation of exterior appetites is to no avail without, above all, the renunciation of what is within the person, what he is – which is to say, practically speaking, a person's own will. It is thus that physical rigours were moderated little by little, and emphasis was brought more to bear on interior renunciation, that of the will.

The Fathers detected, in the primary movements of the will, the roots of sin and disorder introduced by the Fall. The most grave disorder was a will centred away from the love of God and centred on the disordered love of the self. Among the vices, it was not the one in which the body connives that was recognised as the most to be feared. But pride, pride entrenched in the inmost spirit where lies the true dignity of the human person – this was the adversary which lived on, where the other vices appeared to have been overwhelmed, and which could feed itself precisely on their destruction.

Aware of their weakness before such an enemy, the novice-monks looked for help from an experienced monk. Obedience is above all the corollary of the opening of the heart in spiritual direction, the witness of the disciple's confidence in the 'father' whom he has freely chosen.

We know that the solitude of the first anchorites in Egypt was, in general, relative. They formed little colonies gathered around an elder, living witness to the tradition that he tried to transmit to them. Obedience was not established for them by an institution, or through a defined community organism. It was an element of interior perfection and was identified in practice with humility, of which it was a fruit as well as a touchstone. Its primordial importance in the spirituality of the desert came from the clearly recognised fact that pride is the most formidable adversary, capable of robbing the solitary's asceticism of all value.

The collections of sayings[4] and stories of the Fathers give many vivid illustrations of the fact that, for them, obedience was the incontestable mark of perfection.

The Elders said, 'In those who begin their conversion, God seeks nothing but the labour of obedience.'

The principle concern and object of the Father's teaching . . .will be to teach the novice above all to subdue his will.[5]

Abba Poemen said, 'The will of man is a brass wall between him and God, and a stone of stumbling.'[6]

Obedience is the burial place of the will and the resurrection of lowliness.[7]

As long as we are in the monastery, obedience is preferable to asceticism. The one teaches pride, the other humility.[8]

It was said of Abba John the Dwarf that he withdrew and lived in the desert at Scetis with an old man of Thebes. His abba taking a piece of dry wood, planted it and said to him, 'Water it every day with a bottle of water, until it bears fruit.' Now the water was so far away that he had to leave in the evening and return the following morning. At the end of three years the wood came to life and bore fruit. Then the old man took some of the fruit and carried it to the church saying to the brethren, 'Take and eat the fruit of obedience.'[9]

Whether this is history or legend is not important. The story witnesses to the first monks' conviction of the supernatural fecundity of obedience. Here is another that illustrates the same truth:

> It was said of Abba Sylvanus that at Scetis he had a disciple called Mark whose obedience was great. He was a scribe. The old man loved him because of his obedience. He had eleven other disciples who were hurt because he loved him more than them. When they knew this, the elders were sorry about it and they came one day to him to reproach him about it. Taking them with him, he went to knock at each cell, saying, 'Brother so and so, come here; I need you,' but none of them came immediately. Coming to Mark's cell, he knocked and said, 'Mark.' Hearing the old man's voice, he jumped up immediately and the old man sent him off to serve and said to the elders, 'Fathers, where are the other brothers?' Then he went into Mark's cell and picked up his book and noticed that he had begun to write the letter 'omega', but when he had heard the old man, he had not finished writing it. Then the elders said, 'Truly, abba, he whom you love, we love too and God loves him.'[10]

The miraculous tameness of the most savage animals attests that the obedient monk is pleasing to the Creator. The voracious crocodiles on the banks of the Nile licked in greeting the body of a young monk going to the river to obey his brother. A dead person revived at the touch of this humble young man.

The Elders proclaimed the superiority of obedience over the other virtues. Abba Rufus promised it a greater reward than that of the patient monk who gives thanks to God in his sufferings, or than that of the charitable monk who opens his door to the stranger, or even that of the monk who buries himself in the desert to live there in solitude. These actions, he says, are according to one's own will, whereas obedience abandons every desire, and it is for this reason that it has a greater glory. It is always better to do the will of another than one's own: this is a principle that was not debated among the monks of Egypt. The most absolute obedience of the disciple to his master takes on eminent ascetic value.

It is always understood in reference to the obedience of Christ: in the monk, the obedience of Christ is continued. Two texts continually surface: Hebrews 10:5, 7, 'When Christ came into the world, he said . . ."See, I have come to do your will, O God" ', and Philippians 2:8, 'he humbled himself and became obedient to the point of death – even death on a cross.'

The monk's prayer is efficacious on account of his obedience.

> Obedience is the best ornament of the monk. He who has acquired it will be heard by God, and he will stand beside the crucified with confidence, for the crucified Lord became obedient unto death.[11]

9

Obedience in Monasteries

It was to consolidate this value more effectively that Pacho-
mius, after seven years of anchoretic life, founded the first
cenobitic community of Tabennesi in the fourth century. For
him, renunciation of the goods and comforts of this world
was less efficacious for tempering souls than renunciation of
their own will in obeying a superior and a rule. The principle
of obedience is the basis of cenobitic life, which spread
rapidly to become the usual form of monastic life, first of all
in the East, and then – even more so – in the West.

In the context of common life, an established rule of life
takes on its full value and limits the parameters of the
superior's exercise of authority. This has the advantage of
avoiding a certain arbitrariness that sometimes is found
among the desert elders in their commands (commit a theft,
throw your son into a furnace, etc.), even if they produced
the fruits of detachment and holiness in certain cases.

The very juridical spirit of ancient Rome, and the West
in general, led to reinforcing obedience to the rule and to
institutional authority, at the price of weakening a more
charismatic and spiritual obedience.

THE RULE OF ST BENEDICT[1]

It begins with an exhortation to obedience that encompasses
the entire life of the monk.

Listen, my son, and with your heart hear the principles

of your Master. Readily accept and faithfully follow the advice of a loving Father, so that through the labour of obedience you may return to Him from whom you have withdrawn because of the laziness of disobedience. My words are meant for you, whoever you are, who, laying aside your own will, take up the all-powerful and righteous arms of obedience to fight under the true King, the Lord Jesus Christ.

It is worthwhile to cite in its entirety the fifth chapter on obedience in the Rule of St Benedict. It describes the ideal of obedience as it is generally accepted in western monasticism.

The first degree of humility is prompt obedience. This is necessary for all who think of Christ above all else. These souls, because of the holy servitude to which they have sworn themselves, whether through fear of Hell or expectation of eternity, hasten to obey any command of a superior as if it were a command of God. As the Lord says: 'At the hearing of the ear he has obeyed me' (Ps. 17:44). And He says to the teacher: 'He who hears you, hears me' (Lk. 10:16).

These disciples must obediently step lively to the commanding voice – giving up their possessions, and their own will and even leaving their chores unfinished. Thus the order of the master and the finished work of the disciple are fused, with the swiftness of the fear of God – by those who deeply desire to walk in the path of the Lord. They walk the narrow path, as the Lord says: 'Narrow is the way which leads to life' (Matt. 7:14). They do not live as they please, nor as their desires and will dictate, but they rather live under the direction and judgement of an abbot in a monastery. Undoubtedly, they find their inspiration in the Lord's saying: 'I come not to do my own will, but the will of Him Who sent me' (Jn 6:38).

But this very obedience will be deemed acceptable to God and pleasant to men only when the commands are carried out without fear, laziness, hesitance or protest. The obedience shown to superiors is, through them, shown to God, who said: 'He who hears you, hears Me' (Lk. 10:16). Orders should be carried out cheerfully, for 'God loves a cheerful giver' (2 Cor. 9:7). God will not be pleased by the monk who obeys grudgingly, not only murmuring in words but even in his heart. For even if he should fulfil the command, his performance would not be pleasing to God who listens to his complainings. Work done in such a dispirited manner will go without reward; in fact, unless he make amends, he will suffer the punishment meted out to gripers.

OBEDIENCE AND HUMILITY

We have said that obedience was the touchstone of humility. According to St Jerome, obedience is the privileged way of humility. The latter is the fitting enemy of pride, which is the vice shameful before God above all others, including adultery. No ascetical praxis, whether fasting or prayer, has validity where pride reigns. Woe, therefore, to the proud monk! It would be better if he had married![2]

The culmination of St Benedict's spiritual doctrine is revealed in chapter seven, 'On Humility'. Humility is the ladder by which the monk climbs towards God. The degrees of humility are steps of obedience.[3] The first steps of humility consist in walking constantly under the eye of God, renouncing his own will and the desires of the flesh, and putting himself under a superior for the love of God.

The fourth step of humility is reached when a man, in obedience, patiently and quietly puts up with everything inflicted on him. Whether these are painful, unjust, or even against his nature, he neither tires nor gives up, for the Scripture says, 'Only he who perseveres to the end shall be saved' (Matt. 10:22).

St Benedict will go so far in the ascesis of self-will that he will invite the monk to obey not only the superior, but each of his brothers, so great does the 'grace of obedience' seem to him, and the occasions of doing other than his own will a blessing.

Benedict was able to profit from an already long experience of monasticism, enriched by the contribution of Basil and many others. It is he who introduced monastic vows and established the formula. It is rather surprising that it does not contain a formal promise of virginity (as with Basil and St Caesarius). Benedict doubtless wanted to reinforce the community aspect of the rule by insisting on obedience.

Benedictine obedience is more humane and interior than the rather rough ways of the first monks. It seeks not only exterior compliance but also compliance in the heart. This interior attitude cuts short all murmuring and implies open-hearted acquiescence to the will of the superior, and therefore, it would seem, to his judgement.

The monk however has the right to express his point of view in difficult situations, while at the same time being disposed to obey if the superior insists. This already marks a more humane understanding of the relationships of obedience.

10

Evolution of the Practice of Obedience

THE LATER TRADITION

The Middle Ages saw the foundation of Mendicant Orders, and after them the modern Congregations appeared, founded to undertake a specific work in the Church. In the latter, the notion of obedience is necessarily related to the activity; it is in view of a particular task. The Church has a tendency to be understood as a visible society and the links of institutional authority are very strongly emphasised.

The way of living obedience in the monastic Orders has been subject to all these influences. We already find in the Rule of St Benedict a certain institutionalisation of obedience, and the tendency to emphasise of the role of the Abbot as head of the community at the expense of his role as spiritual Father. In the beginning, these two roles were incorporated in the same person. The practical community life of the monastery is conceived in relation to the spiritual good of its members. It was appropriate that the Abbot, originally a spiritual Father surrounded by his disciples, had control over the material aspects of life to arrange them for a spiritual end. The successors of spiritual Fathers frequently didn't have their charism. The community meanwhile continued and its existence took on its own identity. The Abbot became head of this community, his task being to perpetuate its existence and to guard its traditions as a precious relic. Besides, the growing complexity of institutions and the concern for material and social organisation tended to absorb all the Abbot's energies, his role as spiritual Father was reduced little by little to a generalised and rather distant influence, and enough removed that the spiritual direction of individual persons was delegated to others: confessors, Novice-Masters, etc.

In consequence, the monks' obedience was no longer unified as in former times. It seems to me that we can distinguish two types of obedience. I am going to describe them here, in anticipation of the teaching of Vatican II, which we will look at afterwards.

Let us note that obedience to the superior is the nexus of our religious obedience; it makes our will conform to God's. The superior is God's representative, his delegate, for the two lines of obedience under consideration, but, here and there, this role appears in a different light. Ancient and modern tradition, including Vatican II, declares the necessity of a spirit of faith to perceive this presence of God in the superior or father. As it is a fundamental point, we will try to throw a little light on the foundations of this faith, above all the biblical aspect.

Our primary concern is to deepen our obedience as monks. We will look at our own situation concretely in what follows.

'SOCIAL' OBEDIENCE

The adjective isn't necessarily the most adequate. We can see what we are dealing with in what follows. The documents of Vatican II speak principally of this obedience, the most widespread in the universal Church and the active Orders.

It is the obedience of the monk inasmuch as he is a member of the community and therefore responsible with his brothers for the realisation of the common good, and inserted in the network of relationships with authority. This obedience is in relationship with a superior who ensures the order and unity of the community, and the fulfilment of necessary tasks and charges. It aims first of all at the common good. It requires a responsible subject, who is a free agent, capable of taking initiative, and genuinely collaborating with his brothers under the direction of the one who guarantees the service of authority. This obtains for the whole of life.

This obedience reaches its fullness in the mature monk who must undertake a service or a charge. It requires going beyond the individual self in a way that allows the deeper self to be opened to his brothers and the will of the Lord. It is, in this sense, a form of prayer, of communion with God in love.

This obedience is a social reality and necessity. It is supported in the texts that see all authority, even secular authority, as coming from God,[1] the creator of social persons and therefore of the social order. They are applied a fortiori to the Church as a society, animated and organised by the Spirit. ' "Whoever listens to you listens to me" ' (Luke 10:16). The lines of hierarchical authority are clear, the transmission of functions is made by the sacrament of Order, the domain of each situation of authority is well delineated.

Although monastic superiors are not part of the hierarchy, they are indirectly inserted into it by the sanction of rules by the Church and by the fact that the pope is the ultimate Superior of all the exempt Orders. As it is rather a question here, following Christ, of an obedience to the authority of God which comes to us through human intermediaries, the personal quality of the superior is not of primary importance. He represents God as a link in the chain of hierarchical authority, not by personal transparency.[2] God can write straight with crooked lines. The superior does not enjoy any infallibility as regards the technical efficacy of a concrete decision.

What guarantee do we have in obeying him? We don't have an absolute guarantee. None the less, it is the reality of our human condition that we are guided by signs of the will of God, and the order of a legitimate superior is one of the surest among them. Supernatural prudence, according to all the saints, requires obedience, save when the commandment is contrary to moral law in an obvious way (when in doubt, the presumption is in favour of the superior and one should obey). Faith in divine providence and in the presence of Christ in his Church gives us the confidence that the superior's action, in general, works for our spiritual good, even if – in extremity – God must draw good from evil.

Moreover, we follow Christ in his conformity to the sacrificial will of the Father: he submitted himself to the will of good and bad men, provided that he found the will of the Father there. Obedience sometimes brings us the cross that allows us to be assimilated into Christ. Philippians 2:8 is untiringly invoked by the first monks: Christ obedient to death for the salvation of human beings. Obedience in itself is an exalted religious value, conforming us to Christ.

OBEDIENCE OF THE DISCIPLE

There is little about this obedience in the documents of Vatican II; it is none the less more basic and more specific in monastic life, above all in the solitary life. It is the obedience of the disciple to his spiritual master, an obedience at the heart of a pedagogical relationship of spiritual paternity whose end is the formation of the disciple, his personal spiritual welfare. The master interprets the word of God, guides the disciple in its concrete application, sustains him by his example, his prayer and his affection. As with every pedagogical relationship, it aims to make the disciple independent of the master. Fully formed, the disciple should be able to discern his own way and to follow it in complete freedom, seeking consultation if need be only for more complex problems. The disciple comes to have a fraternal relationship of equality and friendship with his master, no less necessary on the spiritual path – it is never good to walk in isolation – but different.

With us, this obedience is lived out above all during the years of the novitiate and in the first years as a young monk. It is never completely left behind, but, as years pass, it is exercised in another way. One of the functions of the Prior, as a Father of his brothers, is to respond to this need.

As the tradition of this obedience is conceived as an obedience to Christ, present in a spiritual person united with Christ and transparent to his Spirit, the quality of the person is of primary importance. This spiritual quality does not belong to the hierarchical Church as such, it is rather a charismatic reality. The obedience of the disciples of the first monks who were solitaries, and, for the most part, laity, is based on it. It is the recognition, under the impulse of the Spirit, of the presence of a charism, an activity of the same Spirit in a master, and the desire to participate in this Spirit. It is in this way that almost all the religious Orders in the Church began.

It is less easy to establish, in a scientific sense, the scriptural bases for this obedience. The tradition simply cites the texts that concern Church hierarchy, and makes little distinction among them. Where the Spirit is, there is Christ and his authority. All pastoral authority in the Church benefits from that presence which Christ promised to his Church until the end of time (Matthew 28:20) and the necessary charisms of the Spirit (1 Corinthians 12).

From a general point of view, it is the law of incarnation.

Most frequently, God speaks to us through the mouth of other people. In this regard, the Fathers cited the case of Samuel and Eli (1 Samuel 3), and above all that of Paul and Ananias. Although the risen Christ appears to Paul, when he asks, ' "What should I do, Lord?" ', Christ sends him to Ananias who acquaints him with his mission (Acts 22:6–21). From the time the Word was made flesh and by virtue of the fact that his Church, in the power of his Spirit, continues to speak in his name, the law of the incarnation has its full value in the things of God. Tradition insists on this point. The saints, filled with the most authentic mystical graces, do not want to trust them until they have been confirmed by another person in the Church. St John of the Cross sums up this tradition, writing in his maxims: 'God desires so much that one person should be governed by another, that he absolutely does not wish for us to give complete credence to supernatural communications, at least until they have passed through the channel and filter of a human mouth' (# 186).

God loves humility so much! Obedience is a light that springs from the encounter of the disciple's humility with the master's discernment. As this results from a free and individual request on the part of the disciple, it is eminently personal and ordered towards the grace of the disciple. ' "Where two or three are gathered in my name, I am there among them" ' (Matthew 18:20).

CONVERGENCE

Ideally, the two lines of obedience converge in the same person, but practically they are frequently, entirely or in part, disassociated. We will soon see how the Renewed Statutes have tried to recover the older tradition in this matter.

DEGREES OF OBEDIENCE

Spiritual authors distinguish three degrees of obedience, attributing them very schematically to beginners, those making progress, and 'the perfect'.

1. Exterior obedience
To do what is commanded promptly and with all one's energy.

2. Interior obedience

(a) of the will: not to obey solely in an exterior way, but to submit the will interiorly, that is to say, to want what the superior wants, with a generous heart, without complaint, even in difficult things contrary to one's inclination.

Above all to avoid detours to change what the superior wants to that which he wants himself, through manipulation or harassment. 'If, desiring some thing, you work either overtly or secretly to make it the command of your spiritual father, don't flatter yourself that you have obeyed in this: you have only deceived yourself. Because it is not you who obey your superior but it is he who obeys you' (St Bernard).

(b) of judgement: to try, as far as possible, to conform one's understanding to that of the superior, that is to say, to try to enter his way of seeing, to take up his point of view, in order to grow into his insight. This implies renouncing one's own way of seeing, frequently partial and too personal,[3] which requires great flexibility and self-mastery. 'As far as possible', because the will doesn't have absolute control over the understanding (but the two faculties are intimately linked: to want to understand opens the understanding in a real way, as one can close the mind and refuse a priori to consider a certain aspect of things).

This doesn't exclude active participation of religious in the working out of the decision, and even once the decision has been taken, he can – and should, if the matter is important – attract the superior's attention to an aspect which is still a problem for him and which could have been forgotten or underestimated. But be careful! Some people have great difficulty in renouncing their own ideas. Let us listen to St Ignatius:

> . . .for fear that your own will and your particular judgement may fool you, it is appropriate to bring this precaution to bear: before putting forward your feeling and after having done so, you keep yourself in perfect equanimity of spirit, completely disposed not only to undertake or to leave what is in question, but also to approve and to regard as the best all that the superior has decided.

'As the best'? In what sense? The superior, as we have seen, isn't infallible. It can happen that I have a particular competence in a certain area and that it seems evident to me that the decision isn't the best from a technical point of view. I can't say that I see white when I see black. This would be a lie.

Let us distinguish two levels:

1. The human level, that is to say, human wisdom in regard to this decision and choice of method. I should focus all my good will on entering into the superior's point of view, as far as possible. If there is some contrary evidence that (for me) remains insurmountable,

I cannot and should not deny it. I must then go to the second level, which is to say:

2. The supernatural level: in a spirit of faith and love, I see in the superior's order the will of the Lord[4] who wishes, through him, and even beyond the intention of the superior, to fulfil his plan of love, even if I don't understand a thing. Finally, it is to the mystery of God that I submit my very limited and weak intellect. This obedience is a mystical reality, an aspect of the night of faith, the dark that is light, but light other than our own.

Let us note that, save for purely material acts, the first degree of obedience (doing it) isn't truly perfect without the obedience of will and judgement: we cannot do anything well if we do it reluctantly. In fact, it is a question of engaging in obedience with joy and a willing[5] spirit, in putting to work all the dimensions of our unique being. The Second Vatican Council expresses this same ideal in slightly different language.

11

Obedience According to the Decree *Perfectae Caritatis* I

Before studying what our Statutes say about obedience, let us listen to the Second Vatican Council, whose decree *Perfectae Caritatis*, in section 14, ratified an important development in obedience, which influenced the redactors of the Renewed Statutes.

We find there a vigorous reaffirmation of the traditional doctrine on religious obedience with all its demands, but with an attempt to incorporate a keener sense of the notions of responsibility and freedom on the part of the one who obeys, and to inculcate an evangelical style of authority in a spirit of service and dialogue on the part of the one who commands.

OBEDIENCE FROM THE SIDE OF THE ONE WHO OBEYS

Obedience is presented along the line of the general doctrine of the Council: religious commitment is conceived as following the poor Christ, chaste and obedient, in his mystery of death and life for the salvation of humanity.

> By their profession of obedience, religious offer the full dedication of their own wills as a sacrifice of themselves to God, and by this means they are united more permanently and securely with God's saving will.

Obedience is 'offering their own will', which is so much at the heart of a human being that the text expresses it as 'a sacrifice of themselves to God'. But this will, this fundamental capacity is not annihilated; it renounces itself to identify itself 'more permanently and securely' with God's saving will. Therefore, religious obedience, inspired by love, is always a search for communion with the divine will, the will that aims at the salvation of all humanity.

> After the example of Jesus Christ who came to do his Father's will (cf. John 4:34, 5:30; Hebrews 10:7; Psalm 39:9) and 'taking the form of a slave' (Philippians 2:7) 'learned obedience through suffering' (Hebrews 5:8), religious moved by the Holy Spirit subject themselves in faith to those who hold God's place, their superiors. Through them they are led to serve all their brothers in Christ, just as Christ ministered to his brothers in submission to the Father and laid down his life for the redemption of many (cf. Matthew 20:28; John 10:14–18).

Our model is Christ, identifying his will with the Father's, emptying himself, becoming servant of his brothers and sisters, following the harsh way of submission to the Father's plan for the redemption of humanity through the sacrifice of his life.

Religious, obedient to the call, to the interior voice of the Spirit (the primary obedience is to God), submit themselves in faith to religious superiors as representing God, and allow themselves to be guided by them in the service of their brothers and sisters, finally, in service of their salvation, through participating in the work and sacrifice of Christ. Obedience being the substance, in some way, of Christ's redemptive act, has, in us, a redemptive value for humanity, like and in Christ. This is its fundamental value. Let us never forget that, for us Carthusians, our work of service comes down at times to this essential.

IN FAITH

'Religious moved by the Holy Spirit subject themselves in faith to those who hold God's place, their superiors.' What therefore is this faith that drives religious to submit themselves to a superior and to see in him the representative of God?

Faith, in the strict sense, is the act by which I believe in God, I put all my trust in him and I cleave, on his authority, to that which he has revealed of himself. What is the revelation of God which corresponds to the faith which is referred to here? Let us say immediately that it is a question of a 'spirit of faith and love', as the following paragraph says, rather than an act of faith specially aimed at an isolated truth. 'Faith' should be understood here in the sense of faith in God, resting globally on his revelation of himself in the history of salvation and, in particular, on his providence and on the presence of Christ, through the Spirit, in his Body which is the Church. We have spoken of this main point at some length.

> They [the religious] are thus bound more closely to the Church's service and they endeavour to attain to the measure of the stature of the fullness of Christ (cf. Ephesians 4:13).

There are perhaps two lines of service. Obedience is indispensable for the organisation of works which serve the interests of the Church. It is also the instrument of this sacrifice of self in love, which is the heart of the salvific work of Christ, continued by the Church. Both perfect in the religious the full conformity to the obedient Christ.

> Religious, therefore, should be humbly obedient to their superiors, in a spirit of faith and of love for God's will, and in accordance with their rules and constitutions. They should bring their powers of intellect and will and their gifts of nature and grace to bear on the execution of commands and on the fulfilment of tasks given to them, realising that they are contributing towards the building up of the Body of Christ, according to God's plan.

THE QUALITIES OUR OBEDIENCE SHOULD HAVE

Superiors transmit the will of God to us; we owe them obedience full of reverence and humility, we receive their commands in the spirit of faith and love, as from the hand of God. Once we have received the order, we make God's will our own. We are not an inert stick in the hands of its possessor. Our obedience is the obedience of a human being, of a free human being, a 'voluntary submission', not the constrained obedience of a slave; '. . .a responsible and active obedience, equally in the fulfilment of the task and the initiative taken.'

Therefore, to fulfil commands, we bring to bear joyously and seriously all 'powers of intellect and will, and all the gifts of nature and grace'. This has nothing to do with a passive or mechanical obedience which has to be constantly overseen, incessantly wound up again. We give ourselves entirely to it and we can do it because obedience gives us the certitude of working according to the plan of God, to the building up of the Body of Christ.

The text is explicit that our obedience is exercised in the

area delineated by the rule and constitutions. Things which have nothing to do with religious life do not come within its domain; for example, the choice of a candidate to be voted on in a political election, etc . . . Our Statutes give the superior extensive powers, even beyond statutory prescriptions, but in practice, the exercise of this right is very circumscribed, especially by the Renewed Statutes. We will look at this later.

> In this way, far from lowering the dignity of the human person, religious obedience leads it to maturity by extending the freedom of the sons of God.

Obedience is not a relinquishing of human responsibility for life and activity. It is a light that clarifies what the Lord wants of us, here and now, regarding our task in the fulfilment of the immense plan of God.

The one who obeys chooses freely to follow this light – he can refuse. He puts all his energy towards fulfilling this Will with which his own will coincides. He remains responsible for all his acts. He is not permitted to do just anything, even evil, without discernment, simply because his superiors have ordered him to do it (a justification heard so often from the mouth of war criminals in Nuremberg and elsewhere). The evil that we do, we are responsible for. This implies a judgement prior to every order received (to be sure, in religious life this judgement doesn't ordinarily pose any great problem, and the presumption is always in favour of the superior if there is doubt; but at the same time, complex cases do arise . . .).

An obedience thus exercised leads to human maturity, as opposed to a personal anarchy which is nothing but slavery to passions and exterior influences, and as opposed to an infantile passivity that seeks in obedience an evasion from the demands of life and liberty. Through active conformity to the will of God, who is the truth and the good of our being, fulfilled in our life, little by little our will is formed in this school, its spontaneity is purified and coincides more and more with that which God wants, that which the love and the truth of Christ desire, and thus approaches the freedom of the children of God, that freedom of the Spirit that tends towards the good by its own movement. It is of little importance whether the act is commanded from outside or not; there is no constraint. This is the goal aspired to by the ascesis of obedience. 'Love and do what you please' (St Augustine).

12

Obedience According to the Decree *Perfectae Caritatis* II

OBEDIENCE CONSIDERED FROM THE SUPERIOR'S POINT OF VIEW

Superiors will have to render an account of the souls committed to their care (Hebrews 13:17). They should be docile to God's will in performing the task laid upon them and should exercise authority in a spirit of service of the brethren, thus giving expression to God's love for them.

The superior is defined not as an administrator but as a pastor, the one who is responsible – who answers to God – for the people entrusted to him. His authority isn't absolute. It is God who has entrusted him with his brothers; he should show himself docile to the divine will in fulfilling his charge. He can command only in the measure that he himself obeys the will of God; what he commands is only transmitting this will to his brothers, his word should be only an echo of the Word of God. The service given to his brothers by his vicarious authority consists in this. He should do it in such a way that the love of the Lord, who is the source and reason for his authority, is made manifest, as in a mirror. 'Who sees me sees the Father.'

They should govern their subjects in the realisation that they are sons of God and with respect for them as human persons, fostering in them a spirit of voluntary subjection.

They are children of God, through the Spirit of God who is given them and they are called to the freedom of the children of the Father: 'For all who are led by the Spirit of God are children of God. For you did not receive a spirit of slavery to fall back into fear, but you have received a spirit of adoption. When we cry, "Abba! Father!" . . .' (Romans 8:14–15). (Cf. Romans 8:21.) Therefore the superior can never treat his brothers as inferior beings, nor as objects, but rather with great respect, as he should be in relation to co-heirs with Christ, children and heirs of God (cf. Romans 8:17). It is always persons he is dealing with, subjects of an inalienable freedom, whose acts have human or moral value only to the extent that they issue from free choice. If the superior imposes his will by exterior or interior constraint, he misses the mark. The will of God of which he is a servant can only be received by the free will of the religious. Otherwise, the task that is carried out has no value.[1]

The superior should 'stimulate' a voluntary and therefore fully human submission. This can be done only by making the object of obedience attractive, by showing his brothers its necessity or usefulness for the common good, or for personal spiritual profit. In the final analysis, obedience should be the response to personally perceived values: in the best instance, the value of the thing commanded, or, when the religious does not come to a direct perception of these values, the value of the superior's judgement. Obedience becomes a communion, a shared response to the will of God, indicated in the first place by the superior in a revelatory way, then assumed and interiorised by the religious as far as possible. This is a long way from exterior and authoritarian obedience.

> In particular, therefore, they should allow the due liberty with regard to the sacrament of penance and the direction of conscience.

Respect of persons in their freedom and responsibility before

God, in that which is unique and frequently incommunicable, is very demanding for the superior. Very attentive listening is demanded of him, above all in what concerns the spiritual life, in order to avoid every appearance of constraint. Religious ought always to have free access to a confessor of their choice, and feel perfectly free in relationships with their superiors. However – as we will see when discussing the office of Prior – all of monastic tradition and the Council itself, in its definition of the superior (given below) ascribes a role of spiritual father to the superior and assumes a spiritual relationship to be the norm (not exclusive, to be sure) between the superior and his brothers, and a frank opening of the heart. The only purpose of monastic authority, the entire structure of the organisation of the monastery down to the smallest material detail, is the spiritual welfare of the monks and the glory of God. To limit the superior to the 'purely external' would be monastic nonsense.

> They should train their subjects to co-operate with them by applying themselves to their ordinary duties and to new undertakings with an active and responsible obedience. Superiors therefore ought to listen to their subjects willingly and ought to promote co-operation between them for the good of the institute and of the Church, retaining however their own authority to decide and prescribe what is to be done.

We have seen, in part, the implications for religious of this responsible, active obedience that generates initiative. Obedience appears as a collaboration between the superior and his brothers, in a common effort for the good of the institute and of the Church. These are the horizons of religious responsibility. To make it operative, the text adds:

> Chapters and councils should faithfully discharge the role committed to them in government and, each of them in

its own way, should give expression to the involvement and the concern of all the members of the community for the good of the whole.

The superior should encourage and promote the active collaboration of all, allow room for their initiative and their responsibility, willingly listen to them – not with a distracted ear, waiting for them to be finished, but trying to enter into their way of seeing, to respect their personal grace and to see the activity of the Spirit within them as much as in himself. The elaboration of a decision and its execution are a work of docility to the Spirit in which everyone takes part.

However, the responsibility for the final decision devolves on the superior, and his service is to have the courage to take this decision with the always-imperfect light that he possesses, and to risk being mistaken. He should know how to go beyond what would be biased or too individual in his own view, to submit himself to the will of God, aspiring purely towards the common good of the group or the spiritual good of the person, accordingly: what God wants of us, here and now, not what I want. This impartial attitude requires of him a greater detachment from his own will than that required of the one who obeys. The latter should welcome the decision of the superior in a spirit of faith, believing that this is what God wants; he should avoid all objection and devote himself to the fulfilment of what is commanded.

SUMMARY OF THE THOUGHT OF THE DECREE
PERFECTAE CARITATIS

We are all brothers under one master, Christ. But among a group of persons, there must be an authority to co-ordinate everyone's effort for the common good. Thus Christ governs his Church through the mediation of certain members chosen for this function; and in exercising it, the Spirit sustains and enlightens them.

Our community, our Carthusian Church, is completely dedicated to the glory of God and the spiritual flowering of each one of us. This is our common good; all our efforts try to fulfil it. The brother who exercises the function of authority according to the spirit of the gospel puts himself at the service of all. His charism is, in listening to his brothers and in true dialogue with them, to interpret the concrete expressions of the common good to be achieved, to encourage and co-ordinate their free co-operation in the effort necessary for this. He is the first to obey the will of God expressed by the Spirit through the voices of the Church, the signs of the times, his brothers, his own interior conscience.

Obedience allows everyone to go beyond their individual interests and to insert themselves in the life of the community in a fruitful way and according to God. Obedience makes charity effective and gives it a framework. It ensures the human maturity and Christian freedom of each one who gives himself to it generously and through love. The renunciations it requires come from our sin and our narrow egotism. The self-will that it kills is the voice of the person of 'the flesh' in us. Obedience is essentially working towards life in us, introducing us into the life of the Spirit, into the freedom of love, fulfilled very concretely in the network of relationships between ourselves and our brothers, and between ourselves and God in the secret of our hearts.

APPENDIX

LIBERTY AND AUTHORITY

(Some texts taken from the documents of Vatican Council II)

In order to shepherd the People of God and to increase its numbers without cease, Christ the Lord set up in his Church a variety of offices which aim at the good of the whole body. The holders of office, who are invested with a sacred power, are, in fact, dedicated to promoting the interests of their brethren, so that all who belong to the People of God, and are consequently endowed with true Christian dignity, may, through their free and well-ordered efforts towards a common goal, attain to salvation. (L.G. 18)

Contemporary man is becoming increasingly conscious of the dignity of the human person; more and more people are demanding that men should exercise fully their own judgement and a responsible freedom in their actions and should not be subject to the pressure of coercion but be inspired by a sense of duty. At the same time they are demanding constitutional limitation of the powers of government to prevent excessive restriction of the rightful freedom of individuals and associations. (D.H. 1)[2]

God has enabled man to participate in this law of his so that under the gentle disposition of divine providence, many may be able to arrive at a deeper and deeper knowledge of unchangeable truth...It is through his conscience that man sees and recognises the demands of the divine law. He is bound to follow this conscience faithfully in all his activity so that he may come to God, who is his last end. Therefore he must not be forced to act contrary to his conscience. (D.H. 3)

It is, however, only in freedom that man can turn himself towards what is good. The people of our time prize freedom very highly and strive eagerly for it. In this they are right . . .Man's dignity therefore requires him to act out of conscious and free choice, as moved and drawn in a personal way from within, and not by blind impulses in himself or by mere external constraint. (G.S. 17)[3]

For this reason this Vatican Council urges everyone, especially those responsible for educating others, to try to form men with a respect for the moral order who will obey lawful authority and be lovers of true freedom – men, that is, who will form their own judgements in the light of truth, direct their activities with a sense of responsibility, and strive for what is true and just in willing co-operation with others. (D.H. 8)

The discipline of seminary life should be regarded not only as a strong protection for community life and charity, but as a necessary part of the complete system of training. Its purpose is to inculcate self-control, to promote solid maturity of personality and the formation of those other traits of character which are most useful for the ordered and fruitful activity of the Church. But it should be applied in such a way as to develop in the students a readiness to accept the authority of superiors out of a deep conviction – because of the dictates of their conscience, that is to say (cf. Romans 13:5) – and for supernatural reasons. Standards of discipline should be applied with due regard for the age of the students, so that while they gradually acquire self-mastery, they will at the same time form the habit of using their freedom with discretion, of acting on their own initiative and energetically, and of working harmoniously with their *confrères*. (O.T. 11)[4]

13

Obedience in the Renewed Statutes

The redactors of the Renewed Statutes tried to incorporate the contribution of Vatican II with the venerable monastic tradition which we have made our own. This is not a question of theory. The texts we are going to cite with a minimum of commentary outline a great ideal to which we ought to try little by little to conform our behaviour. They are to be pondered in a spirit of faith and love.

THE MOST HUMBLE SERVANT OF ALL

We ask to be received for profession as 'the most humble servant of all'. Before God and his saints we promise obedience. In the formula of profession, contrary to the Benedictine tradition, which is nearly universal in the western monastic world, we do not use the formula 'according to the Rule' for obedience. History shows that this was a deliberate choice: our Fathers wanted to make the vow of obedience in an open way, beyond what is fixed in the Statutes. In these cases, it is the Prior who communicates the will of God to us, as we will see later on.

RETURNING TO GOD BY THE LABOUR OF OBEDIENCE

And if, being human, they err at times, let them not be obstinate in refusing to amend, lest they give an opportunity to the devil; but rather to him, from whom man departed by inertia of disobedience, let them return by the labour of obedience. (4.35.7) (See the Latin text.)[1]

FOLLOWING CHRIST, OBEDIENCE TO THE FATHER

Following the example of Jesus Christ, who came to do the will of his Father, and who, taking the form of a servant, learned obedience through what he suffered, the monk subjects himself by Profession to the Prior, as God's representative, and thus strives to attain to the measure of the stature of the fullness of Christ. (1.10.13)

UNION WITH THE FATHER

All our activity should spring from our communion of love with the Father, the most certain communion, that of wills, realised through obedience.

Our activity, therefore, springs always from a source within us, after the manner of Christ, who at all times worked with the Father in such a way that the Father dwelt in him and himself did the works. In this way, we will follow Jesus in the hidden and humble life of Nazareth, either praying to the Father in secret, or obediently labouring in his presence. (1.5.7)

nd the person of the Prior, and has
erson-to-person relationship. For the so
ve the grace that is given to him, this is

person of the Prior stands the person of th
represents, the one holding his place near to
analysis, we obey Christ. This forms the basis
e of faith and love, which we should have
rior.

s, for their part, should love and reverence their
hrist, showing to him at all times deference and
bedience. Let them have confidence in him who
ed the charge of their souls in the Lord, and
eir care on him whom they believe to represent
ar from being wise in their own eyes and from
their own understanding, let them turn their
the truth and give heed to their father's counsels.

7.8; 2.16.8, the last sentence, 'For though many
are the things that we observe, we cannot hope
them will profit us without the blessing of obedi-
ts us to a principle that gives unity to the
of small observances, frequently of little import-
hemselves. Fulfilled through obedience to the
d the superior, they become an expression of
love and acquire its value before the Lord.
eresting to note that the Renewed Statutes here
ified the text of the Customs: 'It is through the
nique good of obedience that we hope that all our
es bear fruit,' (Customs, 35,3) wrote Guigo in a
rupt way.
are other virtues (poverty, humility, fraternal
tc.) that can motivate and make our acts meri-
And obedience itself is not an absolute: it has no

TOTAL GIFT: TOTAL DISPOSSESSION OF ONE'S OWN WILL THROUGH PROFESSION

> The one received knows himself by the Profession made to be so much a stranger to the things of the world that he has no power over anything at all, not even over his own self, without the permission of his Prior. For, as all who wish to live according to a rule must observe obedience with great zeal, we, in the measure that the way of life we have embraced is more exacting and more austere, must observe it the more ardently and carefully; lest if – which God avert! – obedience is lacking, such great labours may well go unrewarded. It is for this reason that Samuel says, 'To obey is better than sacrifice, and to heed than the fat of rams.' (1.10.11)

The vow of obedience accomplishes a self-dispossession, a radical renunciation of living according to our own will. The professed no longer has power over anything, not even his own person, without the permission of his Prior. He has given the tree, the fruits no longer belong to him. He should show himself to be completely at the disposal[2] of the will of God expressed through the voice of his superior. 'Speak, Lord, for your servant is listening' (1 Samuel 3:9). Obedience is essential for all religious life, but the solitary needs it more than others. He needs a rule of life, and in cell no one is watching him. Guigo, like Peter Damien, takes a position on this going against the current of opinion that holds that the hermit owes obedience only to God directly (for example, Richard Rolle and Grimlach). The Carthusian chooses to live under an austere rule; he should conform to it through an attentive and religious obedience, a service of love. Otherwise, he only deludes himself and wastes his time. If, instead of the sacrifice asked by God, he insists on giving him something else, however pious, however costly, according to his own idea and his own will, it is worthless.

Saul received his mission to exterminate the Amalekites, to destroy them utterly killing every living being (1 Samuel 15:2–3) (let us pass over the customs of that age). He defeated the Amalekites, but saved the king and the choicest animals, not for himself but to sacrifice to God. 'I obeyed Yahweh,' he said to Samuel, 'I have carried out the Lord's instructions' (v. 13). But he had changed God's command according to his own idea. Samuel's response comes like a flash. You follow God's will or you follow your own. Saul rejected the Lord's word; he in turn will be rejected.

> 'Has the Lord as great delight in burnt offerings and
>   sacrifices as in obedience to the voice of the Lord?
> Surely, to obey is better than sacrifice,
>   and to heed than the fat of rams.' (1 Samuel 15:22)

Let it be very clear that it doesn't exclude the spontaneity of a generous heart who submits his initiative to the superior's judgement, but only a subtle self-seeking and often the indiscretion of one's own will, the affirmation of one's little ego: there are people who seem generous as long as they can act in their own way with independence; the same acts under obedience seem uninteresting. It is doing their own will, not God's, that pleases them.

> Why do you claim ownership of yourself rather than of some person or land, when nothing in you is any more your handiwork than anything in them is? By what right do you claim for yourself any of the things you have not created any more than you created yourself? (Guigo, Meditation 8)[3]

OBEDIENCE

No one is t
above those p
edge and app
someone to h
thing else wha
impose someth
right to refuse,
in reality resist
holds in our reg
the things that v
them will profit
(1.7.8; 2.16.8)

This important text
(35,3). It treats of pe
Observance in these n
enough. To take on
another context, is ofte
Prior must be sought.[4]
impose some relaxation
today – or a task contrar
has the right to commar
require something more
scribed in the Statutes, b
(4.35.3), for example, to l
astery.

The Statutes seem to wa
the Prior's part, in the m
general[5] (4.35.6 – he does r
themselves, he is their minist
freedom to respond to the ne
each one as is appropriate. I
dition, not the dead letter. O

articulated arou
flexibility of a p
who can only l
important.

Behind the
Lord whom he
us. In the fina
of the attitud
towards the P

The monk
Prior in C
humble ol
has assun
cast all th
Christ. F
relying o
hearts to
(3.23.10

Earlier, in 1
and diverse
that any of
ence', poin
multiplicity
ance in th
Statutes a
embodied

It is int
have mod
sole and u
observanc
slightly al

There
charity,
torious.

TOTAL GIFT: TOTAL DISPOSSESSION OF ONE'S OWN WILL THROUGH PROFESSION

> The one received knows himself by the Profession made to be so much a stranger to the things of the world that he has no power over anything at all, not even over his own self, without the permission of his Prior. For, as all who wish to live according to a rule must observe obedience with great zeal, we, in the measure that the way of life we have embraced is more exacting and more austere, must observe it the more ardently and carefully; lest if – which God avert! – obedience is lacking, such great labours may well go unrewarded. It is for this reason that Samuel says, 'To obey is better than sacrifice, and to heed than the fat of rams.' (1.10.11)

The vow of obedience accomplishes a self-dispossession, a radical renunciation of living according to our own will. The professed no longer has power over anything, not even his own person, without the permission of his Prior. He has given the tree, the fruits no longer belong to him. He should show himself to be completely at the disposal[2] of the will of God expressed through the voice of his superior. 'Speak, Lord, for your servant is listening' (1 Samuel 3:9). Obedience is essential for all religious life, but the solitary needs it more than others. He needs a rule of life, and in cell no one is watching him. Guigo, like Peter Damien, takes a position on this going against the current of opinion that holds that the hermit owes obedience only to God directly (for example, Richard Rolle and Grimlach). The Carthusian chooses to live under an austere rule; he should conform to it through an attentive and religious obedience, a service of love. Otherwise, he only deludes himself and wastes his time. If, instead of the sacrifice asked by God, he insists on giving him something else, however pious, however costly, according to his own idea and his own will, it is worthless.

Saul received his mission to exterminate the Amalekites, to destroy them utterly killing every living being (1 Samuel 15:2-3) (let us pass over the customs of that age). He defeated the Amalekites, but saved the king and the choicest animals, not for himself but to sacrifice to God. 'I obeyed Yahweh,' he said to Samuel, 'I have carried out the Lord's instructions' (v. 13). But he had changed God's command according to his own idea. Samuel's response comes like a flash. You follow God's will or you follow your own. Saul rejected the Lord's word; he in turn will be rejected.

> 'Has the Lord as great delight in burnt offerings and
>   sacrifices as in obedience to the voice of the Lord?
> Surely, to obey is better than sacrifice,
>   and to heed than the fat of rams.' (1 Samuel 15:22)

Let it be very clear that it doesn't exclude the spontaneity of a generous heart who submits his initiative to the superior's judgement, but only a subtle self-seeking and often the indiscretion of one's own will, the affirmation of one's little ego: there are people who seem generous as long as they can act in their own way with independence; the same acts under obedience seem uninteresting. It is doing their own will, not God's, that pleases them.

> Why do you claim ownership of yourself rather than of some person or land, when nothing in you is any more your handiwork than anything in them is? By what right do you claim for yourself any of the things you have not created any more than you created yourself? (Guigo, Meditation 8)[3]

OBEDIENCE TO CHRIST IN THE PERSON OF THE PRIOR

No one is to indulge in penitential practices over and above those prescribed by the Statutes without the knowledge and approval of the Prior. But, if the Prior wishes someone to have some additional food or sleep or anything else whatsoever, or, on the contrary, if he wishes to impose something difficult and burdensome, we have no right to refuse, lest, in resisting him, we are found to be in reality resisting not him but God, whose place he holds in our regard. For though many and diverse are the things that we observe, we cannot hope that any of them will profit us without the blessing of obedience. (1.7.8; 2.16.8)

This important text comes from the Customs of Guigo (35,3). It treats of penitential practices (fasts, vigils, etc.). Observance in these matters forms a whole and is normally enough. To take on alien practices, perhaps effective in another context, is often imprudent. The permission of the Prior must be sought.[4] On the other hand, the Prior may impose some relaxation (for example, either a penance – rare today – or a task contrary to our taste). The Prior therefore has the right to command *praeter regulam*, that is to say, to require something more or less than the observance prescribed in the Statutes, but not contrary to this observance (4.35.3), for example, to live permanently outside the monastery.

The Statutes seem to want to avoid anything arbitrary on the Prior's part, in the modification of the observance in general[5] (4.35.6 – he does not have power over the Statutes themselves, he is their minister), while leaving him with great freedom to respond to the needs of persons, and to adapt to each one as is appropriate. It is a question of a living tradition, not the dead letter. Our obedience to the Statutes is

articulated around the person of the Prior, and has all the
flexibility of a person-to-person relationship. For the solitary
who can only live the grace that is given to him, this is very
important.

Behind the person of the Prior stands the person of the
Lord whom he represents, the one holding his place near to
us. In the final analysis, we obey Christ. This forms the basis
of the attitude of faith and love, which we should have
towards the Prior.

> The monks, for their part, should love and reverence their
> Prior in Christ, showing to him at all times deference and
> humble obedience. Let them have confidence in him who
> has assumed the charge of their souls in the Lord, and
> cast all their care on him whom they believe to represent
> Christ. Far from being wise in their own eyes and from
> relying on their own understanding, let them turn their
> hearts to the truth and give heed to their father's counsels.
> (3.23.10)

Earlier, in 1.7.8; 2.16.8, the last sentence, 'For though many
and diverse are the things that we observe, we cannot hope
that any of them will profit us without the blessing of obedience', points us to a principle that gives unity to the
multiplicity of small observances, frequently of little importance in themselves. Fulfilled through obedience to the
Statutes and the superior, they become an expression of
embodied love and acquire its value before the Lord.

It is interesting to note that the Renewed Statutes here
have modified the text of the Customs: 'It is through the
sole and unique good of obedience that we hope that all our
observances bear fruit,' (Customs, 35,3) wrote Guigo in a
slightly abrupt way.

There are other virtues (poverty, humility, fraternal
charity, etc.) that can motivate and make our acts meri-
torious. And obedience itself is not an absolute: it has no

supernatural value unless it expresses love. Elsewhere, Guigo strongly affirms (Meditation 390) that the love of God should be 'the entire and only cause of all human actions and movements, whether spiritual or physical, down to the least wink of the eye or movement of the finger.'[6] In this concern for love of others, one of his 'Meditations' (no. 433) curiously reproduces the same structure as the sentence on obedience, but substituting the word 'love': 'Although there are many and divers things which a person should do for his fellow human beings, they should nevertheless be done not with many and divers intentions, but only with one; and that is the love that seeks their good.'[7]

The source of the multiform up-welling of the spiritual life is love. Perhaps Guigo wanted to affirm that the role of obedience is to be the guardian and light of it, defining the ground and the direction of love's activity. Thus the modified text affirms, 'for though many and diverse are the things that we observe, we cannot hope that any of them will profit us without the blessing of obedience.'

THE QUALITIES OF OUR OBEDIENCE: HUMILITY, PATIENCE, LOVE

Of you, dearest lay brothers, I say: 'My soul proclaims the greatness of the Lord,' because I see the richness of his mercy towards you. For we rejoice that the mighty God himself – since you are ignorant of letters – is writing directly on your hearts, not only love but also knowledge of his holy law. Indeed, what you love, what you know, is shown by what you do. It is clear that you are wisely harvesting Sacred Scripture's sweetest and most life-giving fruit, since you observe with great care and zeal true obedience. For true obedience, which is the carrying out of God's commands, the key to the whole spiritual life, and the guarantee of its authenticity, is never found without deep humility and outstanding patience, and is always accompanied by pure love for God and true charity. Continue, therefore, my brothers, in the state that you have attained. (Letter of St Bruno, II, 9)

This precious text of St Bruno shows the primary importance of obedience. 'For true obedience, which is the carrying out of God's commands, the key to the whole spiritual life . . .'. For Bruno it is inseparable from a chaste love of the Lord and an authentic charity: 'pure love for God and true charity'; it is the fruit of love, the Word of God, welcomed in truth, taking flesh in our concrete acts; it is always encountered in the company of its sisters, humility and patience. We have here a summary of the whole monastic tradition, a sure way to God.

WILLING AND JOYOUS OBEDIENCE: LIBERTY OF SPIRIT

The Prior can always impose on a Father some task or service for the common good. This we accept willingly and with the joy of love; for on the day of our Profession we asked to be received as the most humble servant of all. When a cloister monk is entrusted with some task, it should always be such as can be done with liberty of spirit, and without anxiety concerning profit or meeting a deadline. For it is fitting that the solitary, whose attention is fixed not so much on the work itself as on the goal he is aiming at, should at all times be able to keep his heart watchful. However, that a monk may remain tranquil and healthy in solitude, it will often be advisable that he have a certain liberty in arranging his work. (1.5.5)

Let us show promptness and joy – the Lord loves the one who gives joyously – in doing what is asked of us, knowing how to subordinate our personal preferences to the common good of all. Plenty of room is left to our responsibility to organise our work in such a way that we can do it in union with the Lord, in peace and recollection. This does not exclude serious work well done – on the contrary, we work for the Lord and our brothers – but everything should be done in peace, calmly, in the Lord, without our having to leave a contemplative atmosphere.

ACTIVE OBEDIENCE: COLLABORATION IN REALISING THE COMMON GOOD

Let him who is appointed to some office obey the command with simplicity, realising that by resisting he would offend, not only against obedience, but also sometimes against charity towards the Prior, who is often burdened with heavy cares. In the Prior's decision he should recognise a sign of God's will, accept the charge committed to him, and co-operate with the Prior to the best of his ability, in the knowledge that he is contributing to the building up of the Body of Christ in accordance with God's plan. (3.23.18)

We shouldn't forget that the Prior is our brother in Christ, a person, and not only an authority figure. Human consideration and true charity should govern our relationship with him – not attitudes of adolescent revolt or intractable and egotistical independence. We belong to Christ, not to ourselves. Our time, our activity, are all at his disposal. The same attitude is appropriate to the Brothers, who are not passive executors, but responsible adults.

The Brothers manage their obediences, and everything belonging to them, in accordance with the directions of the Prior and the Procurator, applying to the work committed to them their natural powers and gifts of grace. By this obedience their liberty of sons of God is developed, and by their willing service they contribute to the building up of the Body of Christ in accordance with God's plan. (2.15.3)

ATTENTION TO PERSONS

A true collaboration requires a dialogue between the superior and the subjects concerned, not only to facilitate the execution of the task, but also to develop a decision; everything in an atmosphere of deference and respect.

Before deciding anything in a matter of importance belonging to the obedience of one of his Officers, the Prior should consult him and try to reach a decision by common consent with him. The Officers, however, are always to accept his decisions with filial submission. (3.23.19)

And for the Brothers:

The Procurator in regard to the Brothers, as also the head of an obedience in regard to his assistant, should exercise authority in a spirit of service, thereby portraying the love with which God loves them; they should readily consult them or give them a hearing, keeping for themselves, however, the right finally to decide and order what is to be done; thus in the discharge of their duties, all co-operate together through an obedience that is active and entirely penetrated by love. (2.15.4)

In general, in organising our work, we can be attentive in the first place to the task to be accomplished or, rather, to the persons concerned. Recent socio-psychological studies have established that even at the level of material output, organisation centred on the person is more efficient. For us, the primordial object of our activities is the spiritual and human welfare of persons. The superior should be attentive to his collaborators, above all as persons, brothers, monks consecrated to God. The tasks will be done all the better. If they aren't, never mind!

RESPONSIBLE AND LOYAL OBEDIENCE TO THE STATUTES

For their part, the monks should give obedience to the Statutes, as responsible persons, not serving in appearance only, as pleasing men, but in simplicity of heart, fearing God. Nor should they be ignorant of the fact that, if obtained without just cause, a dispensation is null. Let them meekly listen to and fulfil the instructions and admonitions of their seniors, especially of the Prior, who acts on God's behalf. And if, being human, they err at times, let them not be obstinate in refusing to amend, lest they give an opportunity to the devil; but rather to him, from whom man departed by the inertia of disobedience, let them return by the labour of obedience. (4.35.7)

(NB Literally 'by the labour of obedience', but the word is taken here in a broader sense that 'docility' translates well.)

We have, before God, freely chosen to live in the Charterhouse, according to the way of life prescribed by the Statutes, and we have bound ourselves by a vow. Many aspects of our concrete life especially in cell are ordered by the Statutes;

the superior does not intervene directly. It is important that we have an adult and responsible attitude. It would be infantile to obey only out of human respect, as if someone were watching. We are always under the eye of God, and, if we obey, it is to please him, and also because we have knowingly assumed and interiorised the goals envisioned by the prescriptions of the Statutes. Thus we will know how to make the adaptations, according to the spirit of the observance, that the circumstances sometimes require.[8] The quality of our life, the profit we draw from the observance, depends in great measure on ourselves; and it is first of all we who are responsible if it is mediocre and does not reach its goal.

We must be loyal and frank in these matters. For example, one can fool the superior and obtain a dispensation that isn't justified. The Lord isn't fooled, this dispensation has no value. To say that one has permission in these cases doesn't mean a thing. Here again, we return to our responsibility before God.

Let us also note that to set one superior against another is a failure of loyalty.

> A permission refused by the Prior cannot afterwards be given by the Vicar or the Procurator, unless some urgent necessity has subsequently arisen; for this reason, the one seeking it will mention the Prior's refusal, even without being questioned. In the same way, if someone asks from the Prior a permission that was previously refused by the Vicar or Procurator, he will mention this refusal. (3.23.20)

DOCILITY

But we are not alone on our journey. The elders, above all the Prior, offer us the help of their experience and their charity. In all humility we should listen to them, 'in a spirit of meekness', say the Statutes. A certain respectful docility, which is a perfection of the virtue of obedience, makes us receptive to the tradition, and to the wisdom acquired by experience, which is often very discreet. At the other extreme, there are the beginners who believe that they always know better and who are critical towards everything.[9] They are wasting their time, is the least one could say, and they risk reducing everything to their own size, necessarily narrow and partial. The capacity to learn, and therefore to progress, consists most importantly in welcoming the corrections which from time to time we all deserve, and which bring us lovingly back to the right path. To be obstinate about them destroys the process of the monk's growth, and of his returning to God through a humble and laborious obedience.

Another text underlines the need to be open to a reliable guide (for all, not only for the novices) in order not to be halted or lost on the way.

LIBERTY OF SPIRIT

For the continuing quality of our life will depend more on the fidelity of each individual than on the multiplication of laws, or the updating of customs, or even the zeal of Priors. It is not, indeed, enough to obey the commands of our superiors and observe faithfully the letter of the Statutes, unless, led by the Spirit, we savour the things of the Spirit. Each monk is placed in solitude from the very beginning of his new form of life and left to his own counsel. Now no longer a child, but a man, let him not be tossed to and fro and carried about with every new wind, but rather let him try to find out what would please God and do it of his own free will, enjoying with sober wisdom that liberty of God's children, concerning which he will have to render an account before God. Let no one, however, be wise in his own eyes; for it is to be feared that he who neglects to open his heart to an enlightened guide, will lose the quality of discretion and go less quickly than is necessary, or too fast and grow weary, or stop on the way and quite fall asleep. (4.33.2)

The freedom of the children of God is the fruit of a perfect docility to the Spirit: to let oneself be led by the Spirit, to feel and to love according to the Spirit, and thus spontaneously to conform to what is pleasing to God – this is the ideal. The letter of the Statutes, and a guide, serve as teachers of this freedom, which no one among us can presume to possess perfectly. Let us rather try, humbly, patiently and with perseverance, to cultivate the seed we have received.

The last word of obedience is this liberty of true love, and this is my wish for you.

14
Mary's Obedience

Meditation on Mary's obedience opens to us perspectives on a profound attitude that surpasses the strict notion of obedience to encompass the concepts of poverty, humility, virginity and abandonment.

There is no question that in Mary we find the obedience of a young village girl to the laws and customs, both of family and society, of a protected religious setting. The tradition of her people formed her piety, sensibility, and vision of the world. But suddenly another obedience is asked of her in response to a unique word of God, a mysterious destiny:

> The angel said to her, 'Do not be afraid, Mary, for you have found favour with God. And now, you will conceive in your womb and bear a son, and you will name him Jesus. He will be great, and will be called the Son of the Most High . . .' Mary said to the angel, 'How can this be, since I am a virgin?' The angel said to her, 'The Holy Spirit will come upon you, and the power of the Most High will overshadow you; therefore the child to be born will be holy; he will be called Son of God . . . For nothing will be impossible with God.' . . . 'Here am I, the servant of the Lord; let it be with me according to your word.' (Luke 1:30–8)

Mary's response is an act of faith and an act of obedience – they are inseparable. The angel does not say, 'Would you like to become a mother?' but 'you will conceive'. He confirms a future fact, not an hypothesis, 'if you want', so sure is he of Mary's consent because of her fervent love for God. In one of his writings, St Bernard paints a dramatic picture of humanity hanging on Mary's response, since its destiny depends on it. This note of pathos does not correspond to the obvious sense of the text. Mary doesn't hesitate before the immense favour that she is offered. She doesn't understand how this can be, but she has the assurance that the power of the Most High will fulfil this mystery of life in her, and immediately gives her consent. Moreover, she expresses the ardour of her desire – may this be so, 'let it be with me according to your word'. There is in this no sad resignation but the expression of a joyous and ardent vow.

> 'My soul magnifies the Lord,
> and my spirit rejoices in God my Saviour,
> for he has looked with favour on the lowliness of his
>   servant.
> Surely, from now on all generations will call me blessed'.
>   (Luke 1:46–8)

Mary incarnates the entire people of Israel in its believing, hoping remnant: 'the poor of Yahweh'. In the purest language of the piety of the *anawim* (the poor of Yahweh) the Magnificat constitutes the high point of the history of Israel, the moment when, through God's action, it attains its full meaning, the fulfilment of the ancient promise of Abraham, the person in whom the whole life of the people was concentrated in the beginning, exactly as it is in the end in Mary. In her is incarnated the faith of the partner of the covenant, that partner's pure hope in God, because it is in her that we find poverty and humility ('lowliness') at its purest. In consequence, in her this faith is also pure obedience to the word of God.

Mary's virginity is the eschatological surpassing of the old theme of the 'sterile' woman (Elizabeth, Hannah, etc.) who gives birth by the grace of God. Israel's faith and hope must be concretised and personalised completely, in body and soul, there, where the promise of God is to be fulfilled: his physical and spiritual habitation in the daughter of Zion.

Mary's obedience appears as an openness to a mystery that envelops and penetrates her, and makes her fruitful with new life. The new Eve, she consents to it in faith and joy, as to a marvellous gift. What the price of this Yes will be in time she can know only very obscurely. For her, God, the saviour, the faithful one, comes in the temple of her body, among his people, as he promised to Abraham and the Fathers. Her obedience is the active welcoming of Love by a woman, faith in the One who comes to her in his mercy, conscious abandonment to Life, desire for the child whose name makes him already present, but whose face only time will reveal.

The decree *Lumen Gentium* speaks of the 'pilgrimage' of Mary's faith. As her obedience is the consent of her faith, we must therefore speak of her pilgrimage of obedience, a progressive deepening. The object of her faith is the mysterious activity of God in Jesus, her son. This deepening is accomplished in the presence of the revelation of Christ through the events of his life until the full light of his resurrection; it is not so much an action as a consent.

Mary's *yes* is said again at every stage.

Yes to the disconcerting words of the young man of twelve years in the temple, who says he is other, the son of his heavenly Father, and is preoccupied above all with his Father's business, at the expense of natural ties (see Luke 2:41–51).

Yes to the departure of her son from Nazareth to give himself to proclaiming the Kingdom.

Yes to being set aside, in the 'shadow of the Spirit', hidden, silent, almost imperceptible. A single time, at the wedding of Cana, through a discreet intercession, she provoked the first sign. There she is pure reference to Jesus: 'Do whatever he tells you' (John 2:5).

Yes to the teaching Jesus gave about the Kingdom and about himself. She is the one who reflected with insight (Luke 1:29), the one who pondered the events in her heart (Luke 2:19 and 51); she is also the one who is transcended and does not understand (Luke 2:50).

Mary appears just once during the preaching of Jesus and this under singular circumstances, emphasised especially in Mark's narrative. The crowd presses around Jesus to the extent that he has no time to eat. 'When his family heard it, they went out to restrain him, for people were saying, "He has gone out of his mind"' (Mark 3:21). They probably came to bring him help, or at least to persuade him not to neglect himself to that extent. It is possible that the phrase 'he has gone out of his mind' refers to the people, but this isn't certain.

> Then his mother and his brothers came; and standing outside, they sent to him and called him. A crowd was sitting around him; and they said to him, 'Your mother and your brothers and sisters are outside, asking for you.' And he replied, 'Who are my mother and my brothers?' And looking at those who sat around him, he said, 'Here are my mother and my brothers! Whoever does the will of God is my brother and sister and mother.' (Mark 3:31–5)

The attitude of his relatives isn't entirely clear: at least they didn't show themselves very enthusiastic. We can recall the brief sentence of St John: 'For not even his brothers believed in him' (John 7:5), and Jesus' word: ' "Prophets are not without honour, except in their home town, and among their own kin, and in their own house"' (Mark 6:4). In Mary, who inevitably lived among them in the little closed world of Nazareth, nothing indicates a weakening of her faith, neither before nor after, even though everything leads us to believe that her yes, during this period, was difficult for her.

But we understand the rigour with which Jesus put himself at the disposal of his Father's will before every human consideration.

A yes then from Mary to the severing of family ties, which Jesus first lived before demanding it of his disciples (cf. Matthew 10:37).

> While he was saying this, a woman in the crowd raised her voice and said to him, 'Blessed is the womb that bore you and the breasts that nursed you!' But he said, 'Blessed rather are those who hear the word of God and obey it!' (Luke 11:27–8)

The only links that count are those created by adherence to the Word of God and carrying out his will. This does not depreciate Mary, but shows the true source of her dignity and maternity. As the Fathers say, she conceived in her heart by faith before conceiving in her body. In Mary, everything is 'Yes' to God. According to Elizabeth's exclamation, Mary is 'she who believed' (Luke 1:45).

She must consent to let the sword which would pierce her (cf. Luke 2:35), penetrate into the inmost core of her heart to separate it from the flesh born of her flesh. She must consent to cling only to the Word which was incarnated there. The pains of a mother giving physical birth to her child cease relatively quickly. Those of Mary in her spiritual motherhood are not complete until she gives the consent of her love to the sacrifice of Jesus as she stands at the foot of the cross (cf. L.G. 58).

Jesus gazes on her. He sees not *his* mother but the *woman*, she who is life and sorrow and love. ' "Woman, behold your son." ' Yes, Mary has a final renunciation. You are no longer the mother of Jesus. You must renounce Jesus to give birth to the whole Christ. He will give you a multitude of sons. In this moment she becomes mother anew, mother of Christ, the whole Christ. ' "Behold your mother" ' (John 19:27).

Her exaltation at the right hand of her Son will be the reward for her participation in the obedience of her Son, even unto death, for the salvation of all.

15

Contemplative Obedience

Is there an obedience specific to the contemplative, a contemplative obedience? In the sense of carrying out a given order, we must reply, no; this obedience is the same for everyone. In the sense of a profound, global attitude there is, perhaps, a contemplative obedience.

In this sense, obedience appears not so much as one particular observance set out among others, but as the very form of a life consecrated to God, the expression of the definitive commitment to embrace a certain life to which one seems called by God.

It is an enlightened attitude of availability and receptivity[1] to every sign of the will of God coming from the inside or the outside. A profound yes to life, an act of faith in the activity of God in and through life, all of life, including death. Yes to solitude, yes to darkness, yes to suffering (but mercy, Lord, see my weakness); the paschal mystery realised day by day in a life laid out in a succession of present moments. 'Christ in you, the hope of glory' (Colossians 1:27); love that believes everything, hopes for everything, allows itself to be led, stripped, reclothed, that allows itself to live the life of Christ, of Life; a faith that touches something of the silent mystery of beings, that sees without seeing, and says yes to Life hidden in life, to the Other hidden in the other, to Beauty in beauty, to Love, which gives itself in the humble love of our ephemeral days, to the immense happiness in the simplicity of all that is and will be: the rain, a glance, a star, a rose offering its lips to the sun's kiss, you, God.

To obey, in this sense, is to consent to be, to love, to live for the Other, to live love, the life that God gives us, here and now, in the most simple and immediate and incomprehensible reality; refusing nothing, without picking and choosing. It is not appropriating myself, not fixing the laws, nor the paths of my life. Blessed self-abandonment. The clay that laughs in the hands of the potter; walking towards the future in the exalted freedom of trust, carried beyond every need by Love, who is infinite respect. To want the other, the Other, to be. Be my brother, my sister; be yourself. A drop of water in the immensity of the ocean, where beats a heart.

To renounce being the Creator, so as to be the Son, word and praise of the Father, in his very being. God's leisure. Lightness of spirit. Soaring bird, motionless wings. A sailing boat on the water. Arms of a tree open to the sun, rooted in the earth, cradled by the wind. Humility of a mountain draped with snow, patient.

In a wing's flash, all exterior constraints are left behind by the interior freedom of Love. Rhythm of the dance, this or that, what does it matter? Not to run from life into an artificial world, constructed by an all-powerful imagination. On the contrary! Complete submission to reality, the most Real, in sincere configuration to the hard down-to-earthness of the created in its limits of time and space. In this sense, paradoxically, this or that is terribly important. The paradox of the incarnation. Eternity in time. A shaft of light suffusing a crystal. Light from light. Communion.

Contemplative obedience is the radical opening to God in faith, love and joy. Participation in the freedom of God. The unfettered flexibility of poverty. Going beyond my narrow little self. Your immense spaces. Gentleness, humility, a smile.

Where can we find a concrete illustration? In St Bruno, perhaps. His astonishment before the goodness of God in all things. 'O Bonitas.' In the desire that drew him towards silence and solitude, where listening becomes ever more intent, and the gaze ever more limpid.

In the fecund silence of Mary, in her fiat.

In Christ. In him, there is only yes (cf. 2 Corinthians 1:19).

16

Authority in the Gospel

Jesus did not belong to the political or priestly hierarchy of his country. His authority came from his unique relationship with the Father, from the quality of his person and his life.

> 'All things have been handed over to me by my Father; and no one knows the Son except the Father, and no one knows the Father except the Son and anyone to whom the Son chooses to reveal him.' (Matthew 11:27)

Thus he taught with authority, even with regard to the law of Moses. He was called Master (Rabbi). He announced the coming of the Kingdom of God, he taught what is the nature of the Kingdom and how to enter it. He had command over natural elements, he performed miracles, signs that the Kingdom of God is among us. The ways of the Kingdom are more or less the opposite of those of the world. It is the poor of heart, the meek, those who weep, those who hunger and thirst for justice, the pure of heart, those who work for peace, those who are persecuted for justice, whom Jesus proclaims blessed, for the Kingdom of heaven is theirs (Matthew 5:1–11). We are to be perfect as our heavenly Father is perfect, with a universal benevolence.

> 'But I say to you, Love your enemies and pray for those who persecute you, so that you may be children of your Father in heaven; for he makes his sun rise on the evil and on the good, and sends rain on the righteous and on the unrighteous.' (Matthew 5:44–5)

Jesus reflects God's goodness in his person. The Father wants

to forgive gratuitously, Jesus goes to meet sinners, prosti-
tutes, outcasts (the adulterous woman, Magdalene,
Zacchaeus, etc.); he eats with them, shows his solidarity with
them to the point that he takes their sins on himself. The
Father welcomes the prodigal son with joy, Jesus goes to find
the lost sheep, and brings it back with joy on his shoulders.
He heals the sick, casts out demons, pardons sinners, on the
cross pardons his own executioners. Yet he reprimands
the conduct of hypocrites, forcibly chases the vendors from
the temple porch, stands up to those who hold power, reprimands his disciples when necessary.

> Then Jesus said to the crowds and to his disciples, 'The
> scribes and the Pharisees sit on Moses' seat; therefore,
> do whatever they teach you and follow it; but do not do
> as they do, for they do not practise what they teach. They
> tie up heavy burdens, hard to bear, and lay them on the
> shoulders of others; but they themselves are unwilling to
> lift a finger to move them. They do all their deeds to be
> seen by others; for they make their phylacteries broad
> and their fringes long. They love to have the place of
> honour at banquets and the best seats in the synagogues,
> and to be greeted with respect in the market-places, and
> to have people call them rabbi. But you are not to be
> called rabbi, for you have one teacher and you are all
> brothers. And call no one your father on earth, for you
> have one Father – the one in heaven. Nor are you to
> be called instructors,[1] for you have one instructor, the
> Messiah. The greatest among you will be your servant.
> All who exalt themselves will be humbled, and all who
> humble themselves will be exalted.' (Matthew 23:1–12)

Jesus addresses these words as much to those who hold
official authority in the Church as to those who held this
authority among the Jewish people. Religious hypocrisy is of
every age: the temptation to hide a vacuous interior behind

a false exterior appearance, a taste for honours and power, etc . . .

But Jesus is above all a model of kindness, of compassion, of humility and of meekness.

> 'Come to me, all you that are weary and are carrying heavy burdens, and I will give you rest. Take my yoke upon you, and learn from me, for I am gentle and humble in heart'. (Matthew 11:28–9)

> 'Here is my servant, whom I have chosen,
> my beloved, with whom my soul is well pleased.
> I will put my Spirit upon him,
> and he will proclaim justice to the Gentiles.
> He will not wrangle or cry aloud,
> nor will anyone hear his voice in the streets.
> He will not break a bruised reed
> or quench a smouldering wick
> until he brings justice to victory.
> And in his name the Gentiles will hope.' (Matthew 12:18–21)

What a lesson of patience is the parable of the darnel:

> 'The slaves said to him, "Then do you want us to go and gather them?" But he replied, "No; for in gathering the weeds you would uproot the wheat along with them. Let both of them grow together until the harvest; and at harvest time I will tell the reapers, Collect the weeds first and bind them in bundles to be burned, but gather the wheat into my barn." ' (Matthew 13:28–30)

There is also a brusque contrast in human reactions to goodness and pardon and Christ's conception of them, in another very instructive parable:

> Then Peter came and said to him, 'Lord, if another

member of the church sins against me, how often should
I forgive? As many as seven times?' Jesus said to him,
'Not seven times, but, I tell you, seventy-seven times.'
(Matthew 18:21–2)

And immediately, another parable follows:

'For this reason the kingdom of heaven may be compared
to a king who wished to settle accounts with his slaves.
When he began the reckoning, one who owed him ten
thousand talents was brought to him; and, as he could
not pay, his lord ordered him to be sold, together with
his wife and children and all his possessions, and payment
to be made. So the slave fell on his knees before him,
saying, "Have patience with me, and I will pay you everything." And out of pity for him, the lord of that slave
released him and forgave him the debt. But that same
slave, as he went out, came upon one of his fellow-slaves
who owed him a hundred denarii; and seizing him by the
throat, he said, "Pay what you owe." Then his fellow-
slave fell down and pleaded with him, "Have patience
with me, and I will pay you." But he refused; then he
went and threw him into prison until he should pay the
debt. When his fellow-slaves saw what had happened,
they were greatly distressed, and they went and reported
to their lord all that had taken place. Then his lord
summoned him and said to him, "You wicked slave! I
forgave you all that debt because you pleaded with me.
Should you not have had mercy on your fellow-slave, as
I had mercy on you?" And in anger his lord handed him
over to be tortured until he should pay his entire debt.
So my heavenly Father will also do to every one of you,
if you do not forgive your brother or sister from your
heart.' (Matthew 18:23–35)

In two similar circumstances, a dispute arises among the

disciples: which among them is the greatest? The first time, the two sons[2] of Zebedee ask to become Jesus' chief ministers. He replies that they do not understand the Kingdom at all. The sacrifice of love is the key to it, and the exercise of authority in it is very different from that of the world.

'You know that the rulers of the Gentiles lord it over them, and their great ones are tyrants over them. It will not be so among you; but whoever wishes to be great among you must be your servant, and whoever wishes to be first among you must be your slave; just as the Son of Man came not to be served but to serve, and to give his life as a ransom for many.' (Matthew 20:25–8; see also Mark 10:35–45)

The second instance occurred during the Last Supper. The disciples, even in the shadow of the cross, still have the ambition to be greater than each other. Jesus insists on his own example.

A dispute also arose among them as to which one of them was to be regarded as the greatest. But he said to them, 'The kings of the Gentiles lord it over them; and those in authority over them are called benefactors. But not so with you; rather the greatest among you must become like the youngest, and the leader like one who serves. For who is greater, the one who is at the table or the one who serves? Is it not the one at the table? But I am among you as one who serves.' (Luke 22:24–7)

The greatest in the eyes of the gospel is the one who takes the place of a servant. The one who holds any position of authority is not favoured. He should exercise it in a spirit of service, and make himself small in order to arrive at Christian greatness. It is a very difficult lesson to learn. More often than not our reflexes are no better than those of the first disciples. We judge according to human criteria of prestige and power – even sometimes in the monastery, alas! What continual effort of conversion is demanded of us!

> At that time the disciples came to Jesus and asked, 'Who is the greatest in the kingdom of heaven?' He called a child, whom he put among them, and said, 'Truly I tell you, unless you change and become like children, you will never enter the kingdom of heaven. Whoever becomes humble like this child is the greatest in the kingdom of heaven.' (Matthew 18:1–4)

Jesus sets the example in a very solemn way:

> Jesus knew that his hour had come to depart from this world and go to the Father. Having loved his own who were in the world, he loved them to the end . . .And during supper, Jesus . . .got up from the table, took off his outer robe, and tied a towel around himself. Then he poured water into a basin and began to wash the disciples' feet and to wipe them with the towel that was tied around him. . . .

Peter is scandalised, but Jesus insists and then explains what he is doing:

> 'You call me Teacher and Lord – and you are right, for that is what I am. So if I, your Lord and Teacher, have washed your feet, you also ought to wash one another's feet. For I have set you an example, that you also should do as I have done to you.' (John 13:1–15)

Before Pilate, whom he recognises as a political authority, Jesus proclaims an authority of another order, the order of truth and love.

> Jesus answered, 'My kingdom is not from this world . . .For this I was born, and for this I came into the

world, to testify to the truth. Everyone who belongs to the truth listens to my voice.' (John 18:36–7)

THE GOOD SHEPHERD

Jesus likes to present himself as the good shepherd, and this image is taken up by tradition to characterise authority in the Church. The good shepherd loves each one, knows each one by name, and is known by them; he calls, he leads to the sources of life and, finally, gives his life for them.

'The one who enters by the gate is the shepherd of the sheep. The gatekeeper opens the gate for him, and the sheep hear his voice. He calls his own sheep by name and leads them out. When he has brought out all his own, he goes ahead of them, and the sheep follow him because they know his voice. They will not follow a stranger . . .'

'I came that they may have life, and have it abundantly.'

'I am the good shepherd. The good shepherd lays down his life for the sheep. The hired hand . . .sees the wolf coming and leaves the sheep and runs away – and the wolf snatches them and scatters them. The hired hand runs away because a hired hand does not care for the sheep. I am the good shepherd. I know my own and my own know me, just as the Father knows me and I know the Father. And I lay down my life for the sheep. I have other sheep that do not belong to this fold. I must bring them also, and they will listen to my voice. So there will be one flock, one shepherd.' (John 10:2–5, 10, 11–16)

Having entered into the glory of the Father, Jesus ever

watches over us through his Church to which he has delegated his authority.

'All authority in heaven and on earth has been given to me. Go therefore and make disciples of all nations, baptising them in the name of the Father and of the Son and of the Holy Spirit, and teaching them to obey everything that I have commanded you. And remember, I am with you always, to the end of the age.' (Matthew 28:18–20)

And to Peter:

'I will give you the keys of the kingdom of heaven, and whatever you bind on earth will be bound in heaven, and whatever you loose on earth will be loosed in heaven.' (Matthew 16:19; see 18:18 for the Church in general.)

17

Authority in Peter and Paul

Paul's letters plainly show us the sensitive heart of one of the first great pastors of the Church of Christ, above all in his letters to the Corinthians because there he has to defend his ministry in the face of critics. A man prodigiously endowed by nature and by grace, with an extreme sensitivity united to a powerful intelligence, yet aware of his weaknesses, and conditioned by the affection and support of his brothers and sisters, Paul lets us see all this in his letters.

'Urged on' by the love of Christ (2 Corinthians 5:14) he is completely at the service of the gospel.

> For we do not proclaim ourselves; we proclaim Jesus Christ as Lord and ourselves as your slaves for Jesus' sake. (2 Corinthians 4:5)

> If I proclaim the gospel, this gives me no ground for boasting, for an obligation is laid on me, and woe betide me if I do not proclaim the gospel! (1 Corinthians 9:16)

> So we are ambassadors for Christ, since God is making his appeal through us. (2 Corinthians 5:20)

Paul is fully aware that the fruitfulness of his work comes from God alone.

> I planted, Apollos watered, but God gave the growth. So neither the one who plants nor the one who waters is anything, but only God who gives the growth . . .For we

are God's servants, working together; you are God's field,
God's building. . . .

For no one can lay any foundation other than the one
that has been laid; that foundation is Jesus Christ. (1
Corinthians 3:6,9,11)

Each person has a role in the church, according to the gift
of the Spirit, with a view to the common good.

Now there are varieties of gifts, but the same Spirit;
and there are varieties of services, but the same Lord; and
there are varieties of activities, but it is the same God
who activates all of them in everyone. (1 Corinthians
12:4–6)

Paul's particular grace consists in a certain paternity in
Christ.

For though you might have ten thousand guardians in
Christ, you do not have many fathers. Indeed, in Christ
Jesus I became your father through the gospel. I appeal
to you, then, be imitators of me. (1 Corinthians 4:15–16)

Be imitators of me, as I am of Christ. (1 Corinthians
11:1)

He claims an authority over the churches he has founded.

Now, even if I boast a little too much of our authority,
which the Lord gave for building you up and not for
tearing you down, I will not be ashamed of it. (2 Corinthians 10:8)

We are ready to punish every disobedience when your
obedience is complete. (2 Corinthians 10:6)

He puts moral, liturgical and other problems in order with
authority but with what love and at what cost to himself!

For though I am free with respect to all, I have made myself a slave to all, so that I might win more of them. To the Jews I became as a Jew, in order to win Jews. To those under the law I became as one under the law (though I myself am not under the law) so that I might win those under the law. To those outside the law I became as one outside the law (though I am not free from God's law but am under Christ's law) so that I might win those outside the law. To the weak I became weak, so that I might win the weak. I have become all things to all people, so that I might by any means save some. I do it all for the sake of the gospel, so that I may share in its blessings. (1 Corinthians 9:19–23)

He finds joy in the sufferings (of ministry) that he endures 'for you', and he completes in his flesh what is lacking in the sufferings of Christ for his Body, which is the Church.

I am now rejoicing in my sufferings for your sake, and in my flesh I am completing what is lacking in Christ's afflictions for the sake of his body, that is, the church. (Colossians 1:24)

At the same time,

...but I punish my body and enslave it, so that after proclaiming to others I myself should not be disqualified. (1 Corinthians 9:27)

...in toil and hardship, through many a sleepless night, hungry and thirsty, often without food, cold and naked. And, besides other things, I am under daily pressure because of my anxiety for all the churches. Who is weak, and I am not weak? Who is made to stumble, and I am not indignant? (2 Corinthians 11:27–9)[1]

This man received visions and revelations from the Lord,

but he also had to endure a mysterious weakness which humiliated him.

> Therefore, to keep me from being too elated, a thorn was given me in the flesh, a messenger of Satan to torment me, to keep me from being too elated. Three times I appealed to the Lord about this, that it would leave me, but he said to me, 'My grace is sufficient for you, for power is made perfect in weakness.' So I will boast all the more gladly of my weaknesses, so that the power of Christ may dwell in me . . .for whenever I am weak, then I am strong. (2 Corinthians 12:7–10)

The glory will be God's alone. It is in the Lord that Paul must find the strength and love that dwells in him, a love full of tenderness.

> You yourselves know, brothers and sisters, that our coming to you was not in vain, but though we had already suffered and been shamefully mistreated at Philippi, as you know, we had courage in our God to declare to you the gospel of God in spite of great opposition. For our appeal does not spring from deceit or impure motives or trickery, but just as we have been approved by God to be entrusted with the message of the gospel, even so we speak, not to please mortals, but to please God who tests our hearts. As you know and as God is our witness, we never came with words of flattery or with a pretext for greed; nor did we seek praise from mortals, whether from you or from others, though we might have made demands as apostles of Christ. But we were gentle among you, like a nurse tenderly caring for her own children. So deeply do we care for you that we are determined to share with you not only the gospel of God but also our own selves, because you have become very dear to us.
> You remember our labour and toil, brothers and sisters;

we worked night and day, so that we might not burden any of you while we proclaimed to you the gospel of God. You are witnesses, and God also, how pure, upright, and blameless our conduct was towards you believers. As you know, we dealt with each one of you like a father with his children, urging and encouraging you and pleading that you should lead a life worthy of God, who calls you into his own kingdom and glory. (1 Thessalonians 2:1–12)

As he grew old, he wrote to his disciple and successor, Timothy:

I solemnly urge you: proclaim the message; be persistent whether the time is favourable or unfavourable; convince, rebuke, and encourage, with the utmost patience in teaching. For the time is coming when people will not put up with sound doctrine . . .(2 Timothy 4:1–3)

But you,

. . .set the believers an example in speech and conduct, in love, in faith, in purity . . .Pay close attention to yourself and to your teaching; continue in these things, for in doing this you will save both yourself and your hearers. (1 Timothy 4:12, 16)

PETER

The former fisherman, having become a fisher of men, exhorts the pastors of the church with a dignified and moving simplicity.

Like good stewards of the manifold grace of God, serve one another with whatever gift each of you has received. Whoever speaks must do so as one speaking the very words of God; whoever serves must do so with the strength that God supplies so that God may be glorified in all things through Jesus Christ. (1 Peter 4:10–11)

Now as an elder myself and a witness of the sufferings of Christ, as well as one who shares in the glory to be revealed, I exhort the elders among you to tend the flock of God that is in your charge, exercising the oversight, not under compulsion but willingly, as God would have you do it – not for sordid gain but eagerly. Do not lord it over those in your charge, but be examples to the flock. And when the chief shepherd appears, you will win the crown of glory that never fades away. (1 Peter 5:1–4)

18

Spiritual Fatherhood

How can we reconcile the fact that the Statutes call the Prior 'Father' in spite of Christ's explicit prohibition in Matthew 23:9? How can we reconcile this prohibition with the ecclesiastical and monastic tradition that gives this title to priests and holy monks? The answer to this question will enable us better to understand the meaning of Christian spiritual fatherhood.

God is our Father through the creation by which he gives us being from nothingness, and through his redemption by which he recreates us. God is our Father through the Holy Spirit, the Spirit of the Father and the Son, paternal and filial Spirit that sanctifies us by making us children of God through participation in the divine nature: the divine nature which he communicates to us in the second birth of which he is the author, through union with the only Son. These are various aspects of a single divine reality, in virtue of which the Spirit says in us, and enables us to say, 'Abba, Father'.

Jesus constantly used the word 'Father' when he addressed God. The Aramaic term Jesus used was 'Abba', the intimate word with which a child addresses his father; it could be translated 'Daddy'. To a Jewish sensibility, it would have been lacking respect to address God with such a familiar word, and, in fact, it is not found in the ancient literature of Palestinian Judaism. That Jesus had the boldness to cross this threshold was something new and unheard of. He spoke with God as a child with his father with the same simplicity, the same tenderness, the same security. When Jesus calls

God 'Abba', he unveils for us the heart of what is his relationship with God. Understandably, all human fatherhood seems
to disappear in this light. There is only one Father (Matthew
23:9).[1] And when the Spirit makes us say this same 'Abba,
Father', he unveils what is the heart of our relationship with
God. For the first Christians, the word 'Father' was impreg-
nated with all their wonder before the immense goodness
and love of God. But the gift of God is communicated to us
by other people: this is the economy of salvation.

When St Paul[2] writes to his 'little children' that he is
'again in the pain of childbirth until Christ is formed in
you' (Galatians 4:19), he speaks of a real fatherhood, active
participation in the divine fatherhood (Ephesians 3:14–15).
All fatherhood 'in heaven and on earth' takes its name from
the 'Father' of Jesus Christ – and also all fecundity, beginning
with that of Mary and the Church, our mother (Galatians
4:26). This spiritual fecundity is not without sorrow: the
Church is born at Calvary from the pierced heart of the Lord,
and anyone who is called to transmit the life of the Spirit
will only be able to do it in consenting like Paul to suffer in
order to make up for what is lacking in the sufferings of
Christ for his Body, which is the Church (Colossians 1:24).

Ministers in the Church – bishops and later, priests – who
ensure the transmission of divine life through the Word and
the sacraments, have been called 'Fathers' since the second
or third century. It doesn't seem to have posed many problems: it is Christ who speaks, it is Christ who baptises and
forgives in his ministers. He is one with them.

With the monks, the vocabulary appears settled from the
outset: they are 'Abba' or 'Pater' without any need for clerical
status. This does not at first sit well with St Jerome because
of Christ's saying (Matthew 23:9). Later he resolved the
problem with the monastic tradition in this way: apart from
God and Jesus, the names 'Father' and 'Master' are used in
an analogical and dependent way, through participation; just

as we can say that we 'are' even if God alone 'is' in an absolute sense, or as we recognise the goodness in creatures without going against Jesus' solemn declaration, 'There is only one who is good' (Matthew 19:17). Created goodness sings the praise of the unique Source of all goodness. All fatherhood that is created and in which we participate is homage to the unique divine Fatherhood.[3]

Origen introduced the idea that the just are not born a single time, they are continually given birth by God:

> Even as God the Father engenders his eternal Word, so it is with you. If you have the spirit of filiation, God engenders you in himself by each of your works, by each of your reflections; and engendered in this way, you are perpetually born a son of God in Christ Jesus.

This idea of continuous generation gives rise to the possibility of a perpetual participation in divine Fatherhood. There is not only baptism and the sacraments, but the whole area of spiritual growth and education. People who lead a child of God to take a step along the road to perfection can be called spiritual fathers (or, in the case of women, mothers).[4] These fathers lead towards God. It is this fatherhood that the name of Father or Abbot signifies for the monks under their spiritual direction; it is not linked to ministerial priesthood; the first Desert Fathers were, ordinarily, laymen.

Anyone who transmits his own life and engenders in his image is a father according to the flesh. Anyone who transmits the life of the Spirit and engenders in the image of Christ is a father according to the Spirit. In this view, the essential and indispensable condition for becoming a spiritual father[5] is first to have become spiritual himself, that is to say, *pneumatikos*, bearing the Spirit, animated, led by the Spirit, transparent to the Spirit, icon of Christ.

It is from Christ that the person having spiritual authority in the monastery holds his mission,[6] and it is him that he represents. The name 'Father' or 'Abbot' evokes less the fatherhood of the superior in regard to his monks than his quality of representing the unique Abba, who is Christ in person. Thus, if his name signifies above all this 'vicarious' role, if the delegated fatherhood is only present within this relationship with Christ, Jesus' prohibition is not transgressed, except in appearances that cannot deceive anyone. The 'father', far from substituting himself for the one Father, becomes the most significant evocation of him. One senses the intimate union with Christ, docility towards the Spirit, self-effacement before the total gift of the Father's love, which alone can make fecund the father's role, which is an image of and participation in, the overflowing love of the life of the Holy Trinity.

19

Authority in the Church

QUALITIES REQUIRED TO BE A SPIRITUAL
FATHER ACCORDING TO THE ANCIENT
ORIENTAL MONASTIC TRADITION*

1. *Experience: to be spiritual oneself*, animated by the Spirit in action and in truth, which demands an habitual union with God, a life of prayer, a profound attentive responsiveness[1] to the movements of grace. It is also necessary to have passed through trials.
2. *Love*, deep love for God, for Christ, for self, for others; with its attendant virtues: goodness, inexhaustible patience (i), forbearance (ii), compassion, courage, kindly severity (iii) when needed.
3. *A certain peace and a certain interior clairvoyance*, fruits of the order established in the passions (at least a minimum of order combined with a great lucidity as to weaknesses and needs, especially the affective ones).
4. *Humility* (iv).
5. *Knowledge* of people and of the realities of the faith:

- knowledge (v) not only reading knowledge but lived knowledge
- discernment of spirits: the ability to distinguish between the movements of the passions, to identify the causes of sickness and apply appropriate remedies; ability to recog-

*NB The notes on pp. 131–2 that illustrate the text are taken from the book by I. Hausherr SJ, *Direction Spirituelle en Orient Autrefois* (Rome: Pont. Orient. Stud., 1955), ch. 3.

nise the different temperaments and adapt spiritual formation to the possibilities and grace of each individual

- discretion: the appropriate response, here and now, to the demands of the gospel of Christ; not merely the 'golden mean' in the language of Aristotle, but wisdom of the Spirit, which can sometimes require strenuous effort

6. *Ease in communication*:

- the ability to listen, to welcome the other in truth
- the gift of speech and of outwardly manifesting the feelings of the heart

NOTES

(i) Never to discourage anyone: 'to give encouragement and joy to souls in temptation' is the task of the spiritual Father.

(ii) 'With harshness and austerity it is impossible to change anyone: one demon can't drive out another demon. Kindness restores the lost more easily. Our God himself also drew men to him through persuasion.' (An axiom of the Fathers)

(iii) Mercy and long-suffering for sinners, 'not allowing faults to pass in silence, but supporting the recalcitrant with gentleness, and applying remedies with kindness and moderation.' (St Basil)

(iv) The one who comes and humbles himself before them [the spiritual Fathers] and manifests the least glorious aspects and secrets of his soul need not be afraid of being humiliated by the display of their perfection . . .The need to appear virtuous is unknown to them. On the contrary, they affirm, when they speak of temptations very precisely, that they are speaking from experience . . .To give birth in another to the trust that will enable him to open himself, the spiritual Father should be a saint and admit himself a sinner . . .In fact, the two things are one . . .'The nearer a man draws to God, the more he sees himself a sinner.' (Matoes, 2)

(v) 'The most famous of the spiritual Fathers gained their reputation not from studies but from their life and the gifts God gave them on account of this life.' Only purity of heart gives access to the true science of divine things. Profane science in itself is worthless when it comes to questions of a spiritual order. Only the Holy Spirit teaches the divine science. However, many among the greatest 'engaged in experimental psychology, even psychoanalysis, in the service of discernment of spirits: thus Origen, Evagrius Ponticus, St Nilus, Diadochus, Macarius, to name the most original . . .They held that discernment is a gift of God, but they understood better than others that God's gifts do not dispense us from hard work with our human faculties.'

AUTHORITY IN THE HISTORY OF THE CHURCH

Has the Church always been equal to the evangelical notion of authority? This is difficult to assert. Very early, already at the time of Constantine, the weight of structures and cultural influence exerted pressure on the exercise of authority in the Church. Vatican Council II, resolutely returning to the idea of authority-as-service, tried to correct an age-old idea of ecclesiastical authority which was unduly juridical and legalistic.

It is clear that in the past the Church has sometimes, here and there, decided to align itself with the prevailing

THE ONE WHO SERVES

The Prior, following the example of Christ, is among his brothers as one who serves. He guides them according to the spirit of the Gospel and the traditions of the Order, which he himself has received. To all by word and by life he strives to be of benefit; in particular to the cloister monks, from whose number he has been taken, he should offer an example of peaceful repose, stability, solitude, and all the other observances of their life. (3.23.5)

...en from among his brothers, *primus inter pares*, without ...exterior mark to distinguish him, he serves them ...rding to the spirit of the gospel which excludes any ...de of domination, as we have seen.

...e liturgy of Mandatum on Holy Thursday expresses ...a very beautiful way. After the example of Christ, the ...washes and kisses the feet of the monks – as also does ...ovice-Master for the postulants at the beginning of ...ostulancy.

...s own way, Guigo echoes the gospel:

...Lord has deputed you to be the servant of your ...let your effort be that they do, not what you like, ...hat profits them. It is for you to adapt yourself to ...utility, not bend them to your will; for they have ...entrusted to your care, not for you to preside over, ...that you may be of use to them. (Meditation 346 ...3.23.25)

...strives to be useful to all by his word and life.' I ...said: 'by his life and by the word which proceeds ...e teaching is worth only what the life is worth. ...ould be first of all a Carthusian, a man of prayer.

sociological notion of authority. Imperialism, totalitarianism, the system of absolute monarchy, feudalism and today democracy and socialism, have influenced ecclesial sociology – and above all the men of the Church, who were, inevitably, men of their age – and have somewhat obscured the mystery. Many are the centuries during which the Church marched united, frequently too united, with such and such form of government, imposed by the cultural situation in which it was incarnated. It is not surprising that the evangelical ideal became more or less tainted by the behaviour of these forms of government, all the more so as the existence of feudalism, investitures and pontifical temporal power meant that the Church of the Middle Ages found itself intimately implicated in political life.

For its part, the post-Tridentine reaction against Protestantism and other excesses led to the rather partial declaration of the Church as a mechanism of hierarchical mediation (that is to say the powers and primacy of the See of Rome), in brief a 'hierarchiology'. By contrast, the two participants between which this mediation took place, the Holy Spirit on the one hand, and the community of the faithful or the religious subject on the other, were rather passed over in silence. Vatican II wished to redress this position.

Undoubtedly there have always been great pastors who remained true to evangelical inspiration in spite of all the obstacles of their times. None the less, the influences we have mentioned have, in general, made themselves more or less felt in the style of authority in the Church and, also undoubtedly, in the charterhouse. The Priors have been fashioned by their times. The accents of a Guigo and those of a Le Masson are not identical. A Prior of the twentieth century has yet a different style.

Furthermore, the tendency to enlarge the houses (thirteen cells in the time of Guigo, thirty-five in our day at the Grande

Chartreuse – see also Valsainte, Miraflores, Jerez, Parkminster, etc.) has added to the administrative role of the Prior considerably, and reduced the familial intimacy of the original little group – although a large house has advantages at the level of organisation, quality of Officers, chant, etc. . . .

If we compare the Customs of Guigo and the Renewed Statutes, we have the impression that there has been an effort to create, by legislative means, a fraternal atmosphere, and contact and spiritual influence between the Prior and the other monks; this depends on many factors (physical layout of the houses, quality of persons, vitality and truth of spiritual experience, etc.) of which several are beyond control (spiritual qualities), or cannot be immediately changed (the houses, etc.). Perhaps we must look at the picture presented by the Statutes as an ideal towards which we should aspire as far as possible in the concrete circumstances in which we find ourselves today.

20

Authority According
Renewed Statut

Obedience is exercised in response to au
see how this authority is presented in th

A. THE PRI

A PASTO

To choose a Prior, attention sh
place to those qualities necessa
Some aptitude for the adminis
also required, but this alon
besides, the care of tempor
others.' (5.38.3) So many
required of the ideal Prior t
assembled in concrete reali
clearly a hierarchy of valu
'a pastor of souls' (5.38.3

O you who are choo
me give you this a
will not be distrac
else. (Guigo, Med

THE FIRST TO OBEY

The Prior is a link in the transmission of a living tradition. He is the first subject vowed to obedience. He must obey:

The Church

All who exercise authority in the Order should always regard the mind and law of the Church as the supreme norm in accordance with which the traditions of the Order are to be interpreted. It is, moreover, supremely fitting that the Priors – to whom their subjects owe prompt obedience – should themselves give these same subjects good example by humbly submitting to the ordinances of the General Chapter and of the Reverend Father, and by avoiding criticism of them in the presence of others. (4.31.19)

The General Chapter and the Reverend Father

The first Priors of our Order by common consent decreed that a General Chapter would be held in the Grande Chartreuse, and to this Chapter they submitted all their Houses with a view to correction and preservation; and to it they likewise promised obedience both for themselves and for their communities. In this way, strength is given to the bond of perpetual love that exists between the Houses and between all the members of the Order, who are striving eagerly to advance together along God's path. (4.31.1)

The Prior makes an obligatory request for mercy at the General Chapter (4.31.4); he is confirmed or not in his charge according to the quality of government of his house.

The Statutes

We have seen that the Prior can, in particular cases, order something that exceeds or is short of what is required by the Statutes (2.16.8) but he must respect their spirit.

> Matters not mentioned in the Statutes are left to the decision of the Prior, but only on condition that what he decides is not out of harmony with them. Whether on this or any other occasion, we do not wish that the Priors should change too easily the honourable and pious customs of our Houses, although these customs can never prevail against the Statutes. (4.35.3)

> It is for the Prior to ensure that the Statutes are faithfully observed in the House. His mind should be so penetrated by their inmost marrow that he may know how to preserve their spirit in all matters, recalling that he has been appointed a minister of these Statutes for the welfare, not the downfall, of his brothers. (4.35.6)

The Spirit and the Will of God

The Prior should 'together with his monks strive to listen to the Spirit in a common seeking of the will of God, for the interpretation of which for his brothers he has received a special mandate.' (3.23.8)

This is obedience, or rather, the ultimate docility, intimately linked to a personal life of prayer.

THE MOST HUMBLE SERVANT OF ALL

To whom could it be said in all truth: 'What do you have that you did not receive' whereby he should glory in himself, and not in the Lord? As Saint Gregory says, the more he becomes aware of his obligation to render account, the more humble he should be in respect of what he has been given. The more he has received, the more he will owe. (Guigo, Meditation 294)[2]

By reason of the authority he exercises, the Prior should cultivate humility, before the Lord to whom he is answerable for his administration, before his brothers of whom he is the servant, before the Statutes which he must obey.

If, in the reading of the Statutes in Chapter, it is noticed that some prescription is not being observed, and if it is the Prior who is at fault, the Vicar or an elder 'can, and ought, respectfully and in private to bring this to his attention so that he may correct himself.' If he does not, there is recourse to the Visitors, to the Reverend Father or the General Chapter (4.35.4).

If the Visitors ask the Prior to correct himself, he

> . . .in particular must be on his guard against, in any way, taking vengeance on or showing himself difficult towards anyone; on the contrary, he should give others an example of humility and renewal of self. (4.32.13)

And again,

> If dissension does arise in the House among the monks – or between them and the Prior – before referring the matter to the Visitors, or to the Reverend Father, or the General Chapter, we should patiently and humbly explore every possibility of settling the dispute ourselves in a spirit of love. For it is better that the monastic family itself provide for the preservation of peace, through the effort and consent of all. In such a situation the Prior's duty is to show himself not as one who dominates, but as a brother; and if he is at fault, let him acknowledge it and correct himself. (4.33.5)

THE COMMON FATHER

On this subject, the goodness radiating from St Bruno immediately comes to mind. And then there is Guigo, called 'the good Prior'.

> The Prior, since he is the common father of all in the monastery, should show the same solicitude for all, Brothers and Fathers, visiting them from time to time in their cells and obediences. If someone comes to his cell, let him receive him with all love, and always giving a willing hearing to each one. Let him be such that the monks – especially those suffering trials – can have recourse to him, as to a loving father, and even, if they so wish, freely and spontaneously open their souls to him. (3.23.8)

'Let him be such'. It is for the Prior first of all, to be of such goodness and charity that his monks, naturally and freely will have recourse to him. It is an obligation of the heart, an obligation of Christ.

His care should embrace all and each individually: Fathers, Brothers, novices, Officers, the elderly, the sick, those who are having trials, lay helpers; the exclaustrated, guests, the poor (no doubt, too, the monastery cat). Everyone has the right to his love, everyone should be known and attended to. His charity is tempered with firmness; he has the duty to watch over the observance of the Statutes (4.35.6), and, in consequence, the duty to correct abuses which could arise – but with humility, tact, and pure disinterested charity (4.35.5). So there must be neither the brutal use of power, which gives rise to bitterness and revolt, nor a failure in the duty to correct, a sometimes painful obligation, especially for the timid and fearful, which we all are, more or less. To know when and how to give a reprimand – never with passion and knowing how to wait for the right moment, is part of the art of good government.

> The Prior must not relax regular discipline with a view to being loved; that would not be to guard the flock but to lose it. On the contrary, let him govern the monks as sons of God, and strive to develop in them a spirit of voluntary submission, so that in solitude they may more fully conform themselves to the obedient Christ. (3.23.9)

His way of exercising authority, fully respectful of persons, should awaken and consolidate their freedom in obedience, and not crush them. 'Talking with them simply and in private, he should give them [particularly the young monks] fatherly, even brotherly help.' (3.23.11)

SIGN OF LOVE AND UNITY

We have seen that the Prior represents the Lord among us and helps us know his will (1.7.8, 1.10.13, 2.16.8). He will do this all the more effectively as his whole person becomes transparent to the love of God.

> To all his sons, both Fathers and Brothers, it is the Prior's task to mirror the love of our heavenly Father, uniting them in Christ so as to form one family, and so that each of our Houses may really be what Guigo terms a *Carthusian church*. (1.3.6)

The Prior is father to the extent that he makes the love of the Father present, 'from whom every family[3] in heaven and on earth takes its name' (Ephesians 3:15). After the example of Christ, and precisely in conforming himself to Christ, he should strive to be the manifestation of the Father: ' "Whoever has seen me, has seen the Father" ' (John 14:9).

And love effects the work of unity. The Prior will thus be the bond of unity between Fathers and Brothers so that they form one single family-Church in Christ.

PROVIDER OF WHAT IS NEEDED

As father of the family, the Prior actively provides for the needs of his monks.

(a) *Spiritual needs*: serious books (3.23.15), doctrinal formation (Fathers 1.9.10 and Brothers 3.23.12), sermons, admonitions (3.22.4), essential information on the Church and its needs (1.6.7), etc.
(b) *Material needs*: it is important not to have a platonic idea of monastic life: it is essentially an incarnate mysticism. The material life of the monastery is the sign and support of the spiritual life. The Prior has to know how to ensure the spiritual goal of the incarnate dimension of our life.

The temporal goods that the Prior administers belong, not to him, nor to any human owner, but to the poor man Christ, and it is to him that the Prior must render an account of his stewardship. (3.29.1)

The Prior should superintend the temporal goods and affairs of the House, exercising a general concern and foresight in their regard. He should prudently manage the resources of the House before God, and according to conscience and the traditions of the Order, taking pains that nothing is unwisely spent. (3.23.16)

The monastery is not a commercial enterprise. Everything in it is marked by the spiritual goal of the monastic life. The temporal management should be undertaken in a spirit of faith; this is not to say in an irresponsible or negligent fashion: the property belongs to Christ, to the poor (3.29.19).

> We exhort the Priors to show themselves gracious and co-operative in providing for the needs of their community, in the measure that their resources permit. If they are moved by Christ's love, they will in no way leave themselves open to any reproach in this matter, nor will they, by being grudging cause their monk to err by ownership. (3.28.10)

Note that it is a question of real 'needs' . . .the needs of a poor person.

B. RESPONSIBLE COLLABORATION OF ALL IN REALISING THE COMMON GOOD

What the Statutes demand from the Prior seems utopian and appears to exceed the capacities of a single person, however gifted. Obviously in a small community of a dozen to twenty monks, for example, everything is more simple. However, the Prior cannot ensure the spiritual and material good of the community and give an example of Carthusian life that is anywhere near normal, without delegating some of his functions. He cannot govern effectively by isolating himself, nor as an autocrat, but only with the active and responsible collaboration of the entire community, and above all of his Officers. (The monks of old often referred to the example of Moses with the people in the desert, Exodus 18:21–2.)

THE PRIOR'S ASSISTANTS

The Prior, as the superior of a monastery that is *sui juris* in the sense defined by the Statutes, is a canonical Major Superior. It is for him, with mature deliberation, to appoint, remove or change, all his Officers, both Fathers and Brothers. (3.23.17)

He should safeguard above all his spiritual and pastoral role. He 'does not personally handle business that can be dealt with by someone else.' (3.23.21)

However, lest the care and anxiety of temporal things should so weigh upon him that he is less able to attend to spiritual matters, let him endeavour to appoint to the various obediences Officers to whom he can entrust them with complete security. (3.23.16)

Before making an appointment to an obedience, he should consult others, especially those who have been more closely associated with the person he proposes to appoint. He should willingly allow the candidate himself also to speak his mind, before anything is finally decided. (3.23.17)

To know how to choose Officers truly capable of their charge and to realise an effective and humane collaboration with and among them demands from the Prior qualities of leadership: that he be sufficiently sure of himself to grant real participation in his task of governing, and to receive the contribution of people who see things differently from him and who have other gifts.

The one to whom the charge is given will collaborate with the Prior with all his ability. And, on the side of the Prior:

Before deciding anything in matter of importance belonging to the obedience of one of his Officers, the

Prior should consult him and try to reach a decision by common consent with him. The Officers, however, are always to accept his decisions with filial submission. Moved by paternal affection, the Prior should learn to know them and their problems; he should help them and support their authority before everyone else; and also, if necessary, charitably admonish them. He should not act as if good external order were his sole concern, but rather by his own docility to the Spirit he should mirror to all the love of Christ. For the peace and concord of the House depend in great measure on the Prior and his Officers being in full accord and of one mind. (3.23.19)

The principal assistants are:

The Vicar: he replaces the Prior when he is absent. Otherwise, he has a role of counsellor, he exercises a 'maternal concern' towards the monks, and he gives a good example. There is a certain complementarity between the Prior and the Vicar: the Vicar has a more or less important role depending on the concrete needs of the situation.

The Procurator: he is concerned with the temporal affairs of the house and, in consequence, with the Brothers.

Here at the Grande Chartreuse, the Sub-Procurator takes care of the management of the house. The Procurator is concerned with the financial affairs of the Order and with the making of the liqueur.

There is also the *Father Scribe* who helps the Reverend Father with matters concerning the government of the Order (problems which arise, preparation for General Chapter, editing liturgical books, etc.).

The Prior delegates an important part of his spiritual functions to the Novice-Masters and to the confessors.

THE CONFESSORS

I do not have adequate information on the role of confessors. Until 1924 the Statutes said: 'It is for the Prior to hear the confession of his subjects, or to designate other capable monks to do so'.[4] In practice, what did he do? It seems that at the beginning the Prior confessed his monks himself, but my information is not certain either on this point or on the evolution which must have occurred. The 1917 Code of Canon Law (which gave a universal effect to the decree 'Quemadmodum'; in 1898 it was particularly aimed at the Jesuits) wanted to avoid any abuse of power in matters of conscience and to ensure the complete liberty of the subject as regards innermost conscience. The superior was not, without grave cause, to be the habitual confessor of his subjects, who were, however, exhorted freely to open their heart to him (Statutes 1.7.6[5]).

We know that Rome currently interprets this restriction very lightly. The Statutes of 1993 say simply that 'The Prior must name and appoint several of the more discreet monks to hear the confessions of the others.' (9.62.2) Elsewhere, in strongly underlining his role as spiritual Father, they want, obviously, to go back to a more monastic and traditional concept and practice. There is certainly great advantage in being able freely to choose a confessor. However, it does not seem necessary systematically to exclude the Prior from this role, and it would be harmful to the highest degree to want to confine him to the realm of 'purely external matters' – this would be monastic nonsense.

THE NOVICE-MASTER

As the Novice-Master is of immediate interest to us, let us look briefly at his role (Ch. 9). It is he who is entrusted with the formation of novices. He is the first responsible for the examination and probation of candidates. He should have good judgement, charity, observance, a contemplative spirit, a love of our vocation, a sense of the diversity of characters, an openness to the needs of the young. The Prior should free him from secondary occupations in order to enable him to live and give an example of the recollection and silent peace of the cell. First to be, then to teach.

In the selection of candidates he should put quality before numbers. He must exclude those who are lacking the necessary qualities, and those who have serious defects.

He must make every effort to enable the novice to choose his way in complete freedom, without the slightest pressure on his part.

He is to visit the novice, to teach him the observances of the Order, and see that he studies our Statutes. 'It is also the Novice-Master's task to form the conduct of the novice, to direct him in his spiritual exercises, and to apply suitable remedies to his temptations' (1.9.4). He must develop a love of Christ and the Church in him. His first care is to inculcate a spirit of adoration and prayer, life with Christ and intimate union with God, which are the soul of all of our observances, of which love is the source and the goal.

> He should teach them to give spiritual help to one another in a spirit of genuine and simple love. (1.9.4)

> Although, like our holy Father Bruno, he should have the tenderness of a mother, it is fitting that he should also show the vigour of a father, so that the training of the novices may be both monastic and virile. Above all, he should let the novices experience solitary life in cell and its austerity. (1.9.4)

He will try to accustom them progressively to this life and, particularly during the last part of the five years lived in the novitiate, to the holy liberty of our vocation.

> Novices, therefore, should be accustomed gradually to the fasts and abstinences of the Order, so that, under the guidance of the Novice-Master, they may prudently and safely tend towards the rigour of complete observance . . .So, let them learn to chasten by the spirit the misdeeds of the flesh, and to carry in the body the death of Jesus so that the life of Jesus may also be manifested in their bodies. (1.7.4)

> Let the Novice-Master inspire his newcomers with a singular love for poverty and a deep sense of separation from temporal goods and comforts. (3.28.3)

> A novice is not reprimanded in public; when he commits a fault he is instructed by the Prior, or the Novice-Master, or the Vicar, who, however, is to be careful not to intrude himself into the government of the novitiate. (1.8.12)

The Novice-Master should not isolate himself from the community. He takes part in recreations and every three months gives a report on each novice to the Prior and his Council. At the time of crossing into another stage of formation, the Novice-Master presents the novice to the community with enough information to enable them to make a legitimate judgement and vote on the admission of the candidate.

Through the Novice-Master

> The Prior should have personal knowledge of the novices and supervise their training, in such a way, however, as to leave the Novice-Master the necessary freedom in guiding them. Let the Novice-Master willingly have recourse to the Prior concerning the affairs of his office, and let him teach the novices to have a like confidence in their common father. (1.9.9)

Studies should be integrated into the general line of formation. To this end, the teachers should act in accord with the
Novice-Master, under the direction of the Prior, for as long
as the students are in the novitiate.

The Novice-Master's teaching should be the Word of God,
the teaching of the Church, monastic tradition, Carthusian
tradition, especially the spirit of St Bruno and the writings
of Guigo (1.9.6).[6]

COLLABORATION OF THE ENTIRE COMMUNITY

On important questions that touch the common good, the
Prior consults the community, normally in Chapter (3.22.3
and 2.22.6). It is important that his government be in accord
with the general feeling of the monks and that the monks
feel co-responsible for their community. However, except in
certain cases anticipated by the Statutes, the final decision
rests with the Prior.

> Since, as Holy Scripture assures us, a wise man listens
> to advice, the Prior should not hesitate to consult the
> community or his Council, whenever this would seem to
> promote the common good, so as to associate his monks
> with himself in seeking the will of God. This would seem
> to be specially opportune in matters involving the respon-
> sibility and interests of the whole community. (3.24.1)

> When the Prior seeks counsel, he does not give any indi-
> cation of his own leanings, so that each one may be able
> to say freely what he thinks. In matters that require the
> consent of the community, the norms given (8.9) above
> are to be followed. In other matters, let him follow the
> opinion he judges better and more correct, without
> regard to persons. For it is nowhere prescribed that, when

one is obliged to ask counsel, one must then follow the counsel given. However, if the matter allows of it, the Prior can explain the reasons for his decision, so that unity of mind can be more easily achieved. (3.24.2)

A PLEA FOR THE IMPERFECT SUPERIOR

There remains a certain unease before the portrait of the superior painted for us by the Statutes, that it is a little too idealised. Even if such a phenomenon existed, having only remarkable virtues and qualities, we might wonder whether we would like to be one of his subjects. Too great a perfection can lead to something inhuman, and particularly to an inability of the heart to understand deeply the sufferings and trials of his less-endowed brothers.

Of Christ himself it is written that it is 'Because he himself was tested by what he suffered, he is able to help those who are being tested' (Hebrews 2:18). Of every high priest, the letter to the Hebrews (5:2) says that he 'is able to deal gently with the ignorant and wayward, since he himself is subject to weakness'.

A man who is weak and visibly imperfect, and who, himself, is entirely dependent on the pure mercy of the Lord, can be a more transparent sign of the love of God, a sacrament of his pardon and of his gentleness. The need that he has for help and complementarity, even at the level of the various jobs to be done, leaves space for the co-responsibility and creative charity of his brothers.

I am not saying we should choose someone as superior *because* he is imperfect; only that his inevitable imperfections are not to be seen as an obstacle. '[My] power is made perfect in weakness,' says the Lord (2 Corinthians 12:9).

21

Notes on the Responsibilities of Superiors According to Group Psychology[1]

TWO DIMENSIONS OF THE ORGANISATION OF A GROUP

TASKS AND INTERPERSONAL RAPPORT

A group comes together and is organised in order to attain a common goal. The work has to be distributed: each individual receives a task that is clearly defined and delimited (Prior, sacristan, cook, etc.).

This organisation implies rapport between persons. When two people communicate between themselves, there is necessarily interaction, alteration, transformation of one by the other in a play of energies and constraints. This friction can produce emotional phenomena: malaise, discomfort, conflict. Individuals do not like being too near to one another because each person is threatened with alienation from the other; he risks becoming 'other' and in particular becoming, ultimately, a thing.

VITAL SPACE

Individuals therefore need to be at some distance from each other – not too near, but not too far, either. An organisational structure aims at stabilising interpersonal interactions in a play of social distancing that reduces excessive tensions as much as possible, and is most effective for the realisation of the common aim. Individuals have to be near enough to be in a state of communication, and far enough to leave a free space around each of them.

> One freezing winter day, a herd of porcupines pressed together, one against the other, so as to protect themselves from the cold by sharing one another's warmth. But, painfully discomfited by their spines, it wasn't long before they moved apart from one another again. Obliged by the persistent cold to come close to one another again, they once again felt the uncomfortable effect of their spines, and these alternations between closeness and distance lasted until they had found a suitable distance where they felt protected from harm. (Schopenhauer)[2]

CENTRAL STRUCTURE

In the social organism there has to be a central 'cerebral-spinal' structure that ensures its organisation, and which functions as a place in which affective and directional energies are absorbed or relayed. Instead of these being exchanged between individuals in a direct and immediate way, with multiple difficulties, it is as if the exchanges of energy and influence were effected by the interposition of persons placed in a central position, with roles of authority.

THE SUPERIOR, NEXUS OF AFFECTIVE PHENOMENA

The person who exercises any kind of authority is the co-ordinating link between objective and rational activities to be carried out for the benefit of persons, and the centre of decisions which then will be carried out by persons. But he is not only that: whether he likes it or not, he is also the connection for affective phenomena which touch him, not simply by reason of his person – and this will happen, of course! – but also by the fact of his role at the centre of the process of interaction.[3] Thus the most important knowledge for the superior is that of the rotating fields of aggression, anxiety, and positive affectivity of every sort, which will fluctuate around him, and in the middle of which he ensures stability, thanks to an equilibrium realised in himself. If he lets himself be penetrated by the affective manipulations that surround him on every side, the odds are that he will harden, increase his defences, react in a more or less evasive or 'phantasmagoric' way to the systems of relationships which attack him: in actual fact, he will play not the role of stabiliser but that of amplifier. And whether this amplification be an excessive magnification or reduction, it will serve in any case as a deregulating, not a regulating factor of the system of relationships that exist around him.

For example, someone appeals to the superior with demands. If the manner in which they are presented is not very pleasant, and exerts a pressure on him, if it manifests aggression coming towards him, he will tend to be defensive, to react, and impulsively to resist the anxious aggressiveness which assails him with further aggressions and other defences, by further stiffening his stance. This attitude cannot but feed aggression and increase tensions which are not necessarily focused in the right place. Whereas, if when he is sufficiently in charge of himself to consider these pressures, not as directed to himself as a person, but to himself in his role, he can calmly analyse the atmosphere from which they come and the difficulties of certain relationships. He thus effects regulatory action within the group.

AN OBJECTIVE, NOT DEFENSIVE ATTITUDE

The person in charge who reacts as if he is being personally attacked necessarily nurtures conflicts: far from resolving existing tensions, he heaps condemnation on them. Now a tension that evokes blame, whether it be in an individual or in a group, turns into a profound conflict, an underground conflict which subsequently reappears where it is not expected, by 'failed actions' (not refusal of obedience, but derived from acts of obedience outside of the given directives), by slowness, difficulties, putting on the brakes; in other words, by phenomena that show diminished energy analogous to that which is found in someone in a neurotic state.

Neurosis in fact arises from a tension which has been censured by the individual. In refusing it, he defends against it instead of analysing it; it has become a conflict which he can no longer perceive at the conscious level and which he no longer wants to think about. Repressed, this tension cannot be resolved; it absorbs a lot of energy in the defensive process.

It is therefore important for every person, but especially for the superior, not to put himself in a defensive attitude and to remain in an objective stance, so as to be able to analyse what is happening. The superior has to be able to master his own attitudes and emotions as perfectly as possible, analysing them instead of censuring or repressing them, so that they may not suddenly be explicitly expressed in the complex system of relationships of which he is the centre.

INTERCOMMUNICATION

It is very difficult to see what truly happens in the emotional interactions within a group. The superior consequently has to take precautions in evaluating what happens around him, and the projections he may make of himself. He should be sensitive to the tensions and difficulties which may exist, and from time to time help them to be expressed by an attitude of openness and receptivity in order to try to see how it might be possible to relieve the situation.

THE POWER OF ANALYSIS

From this point of view, the greatest power at the disposal of a person in charge vis-à-vis a group, is not the power of coercion and decision-making, but the power of analysis which he can put in motion by individual or community investigations (meetings, requests for information, etc.); this is operative to the extent that he tries to facilitate communications to the maximum, therefore receiving them with a non-defensive attitude when they contain elements of aggression towards himself. He must understand that a certain amount of this aggression is perhaps merited by his action, but that most of it is the product of illusions, and of an erroneous nature; most of it is aimed at him as a result of affective elements that arise due to his position. He should not, therefore, be excessively concerned with criticisms that can be addressed to him, but he also should not defend himself from them immoderately, to the point that he cannot see the core of reality of these criticisms, even when they are veiled.

BOND OF AUTHORITY

A leader should not seduce. He should not misuse the affective or emotional influence allowed by his role in being paternalistic or hail-fellow-well-met. On the contrary, the goal should be to ensure a perfectly objective relationship of responsibility, precisely regulated by clear communication.

The superior is one who stands, not at a distance, but to a precise contact: he maintains the right distance by refusing to protect himself, by avoiding 'self-justification', and making himself affectively 'gratifying' to his community; and by avoiding, on the other hand, a false collusion – because he is charged with a specific role which he must ensure without either deviation or oppression.

To be responsible is to be oneself, without false identification, without escaping into bureaucratic directives. It is to communicate to the self, bearing one's solitude without reinforcing it, so as to understand better the responsibility of others, without diminishing it. The exercise of authority is not limited to the superior. Every person who improves the cohesion of a group or who clarifies roles among persons or common objectives is an agent of authority.

FUNCTIONS OF AUTHORITY

Authority acts in order to:

— define the objectives of the group
— determine and distribute roles to people

— develop procedures for working
— intervene with sanctions.

This activity should have three qualities: clarity, relevance, acceptance (by the group).

The role of authority is to avoid a fragmentation of activities by each, that is to say, to make the group function as a coherent unit.

The specific role of the superior is to be the guardian of responsibility, that is to say, the channelling agent of the acts which will control the command, in assuring the authorisation of authority according to the order of competence.

To be responsible is to authorise, that is to say, to make other people 'originators', responsible for their tasks by reason of their real competence, for the benefit of the group. The subordinate is not to be short-circuited by taking his place, nor by dealing with problems that are his concern alone or with others.

THE NON-EXERCISE OF ALL AVAILABLE POWER

Each time we have a responsibility, we all tend to absorb into our own selves the totality of power, competence, and decision-making that the responsibility confided to us in relationship to a group supposes. We are tempted to accumulate everything on our own shoulders. 'We believe by tradition about gods, and we see by experience about men, that always, by a necessity of nature, a being exercises all the power at its disposal' (Thucydides). And the irony is that even when the superior does not want to exercise all the power at his disposal, the subordinates want to make him do so: they arrange things so that he is the sole centre of authority, the sole centre of decisions, even though, on his side, he tries hard to give them their share of full responsibility, their area of decision-making, their realm of competence, in function of their role.

The subordinates should feel themselves responsible, in a state of freedom regarding their choices, really in charge, in a position of taking risks. The superior should refuse to play the role of 'umbrella' in relating to them.

When someone poses a problem and suggests a decision, the superior can ask him: 'And do you take responsibility?' If he hesitates and defends himself, he should refuse the project.

BUREAUCRACY

Human nature always seeks to avoid responsibility and risk. The tendency in a social body, which is drawn out in time, is to reinforce excessively the bureaucratic armour. The organism is held together by impersonal structures rather than by persons having an area of responsibility involving a margin of risk.

When a structure is clearly defined so that each knows what he has to do and the roles are well-adapted, everything should work; but in reality there are all sorts of glitches: deceleration, setbacks, various problems. Impersonal relations, which exonerate people from responsibility, do not allow for careful management of human activities. The acts of freedom, the risks experienced and the emotional phenomena are camouflaged and masked; they cannot be expressed through communication; they are censored, but as they are not suppressed they appear in unpredictable and uncontrollable ways by all kinds of loss of energy, frictions, etc.

Owing to rigid structures, the bureaucratic tendency is

unduly to fix relations and distances between people and necessarily leads to a lack of adjustment. A rudder can be fixed in a certain direction to go forward on the high seas during a cruise when the exterior circumstances change moderately and slowly; but this setting would be catastrophic if near the coast and in a rapidly evolving situation.

FLEXIBLE SYSTEM

That situation calls for a flexible system: it has to evolve from an armour-plated dinosaur to a vertebrate endowed with an interior structure particularly finely tuned at the level of communications and orientations, highly sensitive to rapidly changing circumstances, both exterior and interior. There must above all be easy communication from the bottom towards the top.

Some of this psychological data concerns social bodies, social organisms, larger than our communities, other parts of it reflect the fundamental laws of social reality. They have to be adapted to our concrete situation and in harmony with the spiritual goal of our life. They should also be respected as far as possible. Here, too, grace builds on nature.

Lord, make me an instrument of your peace;
    where there is hatred, let me sow love;
    where there is injury, pardon;
    where there is doubt, faith;
    where there is despair, hope;
    where there is darkness, light;
    where there is sadness, joy.

O divine Master, grant that I may not so much seek
    to be consoled as to console,

to be understood as to understand,
to be loved as to love.

For it is in giving that we receive;
   it is in pardoning that we are pardoned;
   it is in dying that we are born to eternal life.

Prayer attributed to St Francis

22

The Father Master of Novices in the History of Chartreuse[1]

(a) FROM THE ELEVENTH TO THE SIXTEENTH CENTURY

The Novice-Master as a distinct entity does not appear in our Order before the seventeenth century. In the first group of Carthusians it was the example and the light of St Bruno which led and guided the aspirations of his companions. This is the ancient monastic tradition of the spiritual Father surrounded by his disciples.

At the time of Guigo (Customs, 22, 3 and 4) the situation remained the same, although slightly institutionalised. The Prior had the duty to visit the novice frequently during his novitiate. Alongside him there was an elder, sometimes one, sometimes another, to which each novice was entrusted. His role was scarcely more than that of a master of ceremonies, and lasted for about a week.

After a year of novitiate, solemn vows were made. The formation was very succinct: it consisted in learning the customs and ceremonies of the life, living it effectively, a few meetings with the Prior (some understanding of the vows which would be made, general monastic doctrine?), and that was all. From all evidence, it was the life itself, and assimilation into a living community, which formed the young professed.

At this time there was not a brutal rupture between the world and the cloister. Becoming a monk was only the logical consequence of the Christian attitudes and values of the age. Even materially the difference from life in the world was not so great. The aspirant to the monastic life already had a significant religious formation.

During the following centuries, the life became more institutionalised, more complicated; the Prior was more and more caught up in administrative concerns. Little by little he relinquished a considerable part of his personal role in formation, for which immediate responsibility lay more with the elders who were in charge of the novices (see Ord. 168).

(b) FROM THE SIXTEENTH CENTURY TO THE REVOLUTION

In 1582 the 'Nova Collectio' made a significant change: '[The Prior] will entrust the novice to one of the monks whom he knows to be the most apt for this, seniority not being taken into account . . .Several novices can be put into the care of one and the same monk if the Prior thinks this would be best' (11.17.16).

The care of the novices had become too important to be entrusted simply to the convention of seniority. They wanted the most capable person and were on the way towards having just one Novice-Master.

At the Grande Chartreuse as far back as 1572, the charge of Novice-Master was assumed by the Vicar.[2]

From the end of the Wars of Religion in 1593, there was a 'demographic explosion' in Chartreuse: in 1592, eight professions each year; in 1599, twenty-four professions.

Between 1600 and 1700, 555 professions of which 525 persevered (94.6 per cent).

The Vicar Novice-Masters (14) who formed all of these monks were in general surprisingly young. Most had an average of eleven years of profession, and so were, on average, thirty years old. They remained in office on average for seven years (but five of them for two years or less). They were competent young monks, destined for the most part to go on to important positions in the Order.

In 1688 Dom Le Masson officially established the distinct charge of Master of Novices. In the third edition of the 'Nova Collectio' the last phrase previously cited becomes, 'All the novices must be put into the care of one and the same monk' (11.17.16). In the same edition is transcribed the Ordinance of the Chapter of 1679 promulgating the obligation to follow Dom Le Masson's Directory of Novices.

In the eighteenth century there were 317 professions at the Grande Chartreuse, of which 295 persevered (93.1 per cent). The average age of the new Novice-Masters was only 29.7 years. They entered young in those days. Young monks destined to hold important offices in the Order stayed as Novice-Master for an average of three years.

It seems that early in the eighteenth century the young religious remained five years under the tutelage of the Father Master, although making solemn profession at the end of a year. They were perhaps less separated from the community than the novices (?). What sort of formation did the Novice-Masters give? What was the role of the confessors? We know little of these things. The Prior was an important factor (for example, Dom Le Masson) and also the community. In reality, it is the monastic life lived in its entirety that makes the Christian a monk.

This was still a stable world, certainties were held in peace, and there was a certain homogeneity of culture and religious attitudes between the world and the cloister. Formation, more concentrated in the hands of a single monk, chosen for his capacities but young and with no special training at all, seemed still to suffice. But already the Revolution was casting its shadow. At the end of the eighteenth century, there were signs of growing instability within the Order, which reflected a certain restlessness.

(c) FROM THE REVOLUTION TO THE TWENTIETH CENTURY

Then came the catastrophe: the expulsion from the Grande Chartreuse in 1792, confusion, the death of numerous members of the Order. The small remnant that survived returned to the monastery in 1816. The flow of vocations began again seriously only towards 1825. From 1860, there was a large enrolment: at the Grande Chartreuse 363 professions for the nineteenth century (266 between 1850 and 1900) of which 260 (72 per cent) persevered.

But we note a change particularly in the second half of the century. One hundred and forty-two of them were priests before entering, a rare thing in the preceding centuries, and the age of these candidates was quite high (on average forty years, several were more than fifty years old at entrance).

We see a world in crisis, certainties were shaken. There was greater instability in the vocations.

The single year of formation in use since the beginning was no longer a sufficient time of probation for a definitive engagement. Thus from 1839, there were two years of novitiate and the stage of simple perpetual vows (four years) was created in 1851. These measures restored the situation among those professed in solemn vows until 1910, but among those professed in simple vows the proportion of departures is shown to be quite important (19 per cent).

Throughout the century stability was much more fragile than before the Revolution (in all, 28 per cent departures of professed religious).

The Novice-Masters were on average forty-two years old, much older than before, but this was not a constant: five Novice-Masters were nominated at less than thirty years, six at more than fifty-five years. The duration of their charge averaged two years and five months; only three stayed for more than five years. During the Generalate of Dom Charles-Marie Saisson there were eleven Novice-Masters in fourteen years! Some were in office only a few months.

In general, there was an almost incredible instability within the Order. Monks continually changed houses (several every two or three years), and even within the houses (in general, the Officers remained in a charge for a very short time); there was a whirlwind of movement.

To make room at the Grande Chartreuse, the young professed were sent to other houses immediately after their first profession. A very great number of young professed had already changed house three or four times before solemn profession. And as the Novice-Masters themselves changed continually in all the houses, many religious had up to five or even seven Novice-Masters in the course of their novitiate. It also happened that several priests who were already old when they entered were appointed to the charge of Novice-Master while they were still young professed (in several houses, not at the Grande Chartreuse).

What formation did these Novice-Masters give when most of them held their post for such a brief period? Their own monastic formation seems frequently to have been rather thin. According to the documents and correspondence that remain with us, the preoccupations of at least some Novice-Masters were centred on preternatural occurrences, or what were assumed to be such throughout the Church, formulas for prayer, 'recipes' for all sorts of special devotions, the foundation of associations or good works outside the monastery, multiple relations with the world, etc.

This gives an idea of the atmosphere in which our houses lived in the course of the nineteenth century. They were too rich and too exteriorised. Furthermore, the constant coming and going within the Order made impossible a real family spirit and peace in the communities. One historian of the Order writes:

> In the last years of the nineteenth century, the deterioration of the Order had reached a very advanced degree. From the point of view of circumspection in recruitment, of stability, of the spirit of solitude, we see nothing Carthusian left at this time . . . The situation of the Order as regards its vocation appears to have been the most critical then than at any time in its history . . . It required the terrible suffering of expulsion, with all its wreckage and uprootings, for a reawakening to occur. (Dom Maurice Laporte, an unpublished study)

However, there were several positive factors. A fusion between the Chartreuse before the Revolution and that after was realised by the re-establishment of the exterior framework of observances of the Carthusian life prescribed by the Statutes, by the Reverend Father Jean-Baptiste Mortaize, after the return to the Grande Chartreuse. In this way at least the availability of a setting for the contemplative ideal was conserved intact, even though the quest for this ideal was undergoing weakening badly.

This policy of conservation reflects that of the Church in general, faced with the confusion of ideas and values which issued from the Revolution. This temporary defensive position needed to be followed by a more constructive and positive attitude.

On the other hand, the Novice-Masters were pouring out meticulous explications of the Statutes on the novitiates. The juridical rigidity and the lack of spiritual impetus of the written commentaries of this period make them unreadable today. However, this obscure work helped to keep intact the exterior framework, and something of the spirit of the vocation. It also ensured a measure of continuity during the years of the novitiate in the midst of incessant changes of Novice-Masters and location. The fidelity of the General Chapter to the authentic Carthusian ideal was also very important. For example, at the time when enrolment in the novitiate was most neglected and formation most deficient, the General Chapter promulgated, in 1893, one of the most remarkable ordinances in our history on recruitment and formation, the ordinance which today forms the substance of the chapter on the Father Master in the new Statutes (1971).

(d) TWENTIETH CENTURY

The expulsion in 1903 dealt a serious blow to recruitment at the Grande Chartreuse, as regards numbers.

1900–50: 97 professions of which 55 persevered (57%)
1950–70: 24 professions of which 13 persevered (54%)

Perseverance is even more fragile than in the nineteenth century.

In 1924, one year of novitiate, and it was decided that there would be four years of temporary vows, then solemn profession.

In 1949, two years of novitiate, three years of temporary vows, then solemn profession.

In 1969, two years of temporary vows among the perpetually professed are added, before solemn profession.

In 1971 the Renewed Statutes dedicated a new chapter to the Novice-Master.

There has been a clear trend towards greater maturity before nomination of Novice-Masters at the Grande Chartreuse: the average age is forty-seven years. And they remain longer in charge. In seventy-two years there have been only seven Novice-Masters, of which two remained in office more than thirteen years and one other twenty-four years. The average is ten years.

All the Novice-Masters between 1903 and 1950 (that is to say, before Dom Maurice) were priests before entering, except one who was a deacon. They could take their task more seriously than those who were Novice-Master for only a brief time. Selection has become more careful and more exacting.

The tendency in formation during this time seems to remain along the same lines as in the nineteenth century: a spirituality based on the Statutes and the Ordinary, but perhaps with more spiritual and even mystical impetus, even though taken from non-Carthusian sources (the Carmelite mystics especially). In the second half of the twentieth century, a return to Carthusian sources, started in the nineteenth century, helped to give a more monastic and more specifically Carthusian note to the formation of recent years.

We can wonder if an effort towards assimilation of our authentic tradition, and of translation and communication into more modern terms doesn't remain to be done.

At the level of the Order, the expulsion at the beginning of the century was the occasion of a beneficial purification, realised above all by the vigorous action of the Reverend Fathers, particularly of Dom Jacques Mayaud from 1911. The instability inside the Order was practically suppressed, and the transfers reduced to strict necessity; the spirit of solitude was revived, and excessive relations with the outside cut off. The Order, after the return in 1940, rediscovered a more contemplative and more genuine rhythm of life.

The fact that all of these efforts have not had, for the time being, a decisive effect (eight professed between 1960 and 1970, two left after temporary vows, three after solemn vows – 62 per cent) shows that there are very grave problems to be faced. They have their roots in the condition of the world from which we come and from which our candidates come, or don't come. This world is engraved in the heart of each of us.

It is a world thrown into upheaval by two world wars, by the appearance of massive atheism, by Marxism, by the affirmation of the person and absolute personal freedom, by an intellectual relativism, by confrontation with other religions in the perspective of a world become small, by an accelerated mutation of culture and morals. At the level of the Church, the opening to the world realised by Vatican II, and the importance given to the life of the laity, hardly favours monastic vocations, with the exception, sometimes, of vocations of escape and fear. The questioning of everything and pluralism in matters of doctrine, and the loss of the Church's teaching authority give a blurred and ambiguous image of the priest and religious.

The young people who come to us are more and more 'converts', coming from a non-practising or non-religious milieu. They have found God through a personal journey, and frequently bypassing through atheism, Oriental religions, etc. Almost all have had some religious experience, but their Christian knowledge, particularly in the area of doctrine, is very poor.

All young people, even those coming from a Christian milieu, have quite critical intellectual habits, a mistrust of dogmatic authority and of institutions in general, a very lively sense of their liberty and their personality. Frequently their intellectual maturity far surpasses their affective development. Formation should be adapted to these people if it is to be effective. Our Order has to show that it is capable of giving them the life of union with God and fraternal charity that they seek, without which our Order cannot continue to exist.

Notes

1. The Freedom of Love

1. *Lumen Gentium* (L.G.), 44, in *Vatican Council II: The Conciliar and Post Conciliar Documents*, ed. Austin Flannery OP (Dublin, 1992), pp. 403–4.
2. Ibid.
3. *Summa Theologica* (S.T.) 2.2 Q.88.a.6.
4. And in many other psalms; see the word 'rock' in a concordance.
5. S.T. 2.2. Q.88.a.4.
6. *Perfectae Caritatis* (P.C.), 1.
7. P.C. 2.
8. L.G. 46.
9. Ibid.
10. P.C. 1.
11. Fr. *disponibilité*.
12. L.G. 44.
13. Ibid.
14. P.C.1.
15. L.G. 44.

2. Religious Life in the Church

1. – 'The monk, already by baptism dead to sin and consecrated to God, is by Profession still more totally dedicated to the Father and set free from the world, in order to be able to strive more directly towards perfect love; linked with the Lord in firm and stable pact, he shares in the mystery of the Church's indissoluble union with Christ, and bears witness to the world of that new life won for us by Christ's redemption' (1.10.1.) (cf. L.G. 44).

    – 'Following the example of Jesus Christ, who came to do the will of his Father, and who taking the form of a servant, learned obedience through what he suffered, the monk subjects himself by Profession to the Prior, as God's representative, and thus strives

to attain to the measure of the stature of the fullness of Christ'
(1.10.13) (cf. P.C. 14).
2. L.G. 31.
3. L.G. 42.
4. Ibid.
5. L.G. 43.
6. Ibid.
7. L.G. 44.

3. Profession

1. It is the will of the Church that determines the juridical effects
   attached to various sorts of vows. The 1983 Code of Canon Law
   omits the distinction between solemn vows and simple perpetual
   vows. Religious Institutes which had solemn profession prior to
   this revision of Canon Law can continue to use the term in their
   proper law, which can attribute to the Profession the effects of
   solemn profession.

4. Forgetfulness and Creation

1. Fr. *disponible*.
2. Gregory of Nyssa, cf. *Against Eunomius* and *The Life of Moses*.
3. Ibid.
4. The priesthood of the faithful is a real participation in the priesthood of Christ and bestows the power of offering oneself and
   everything in Christ, with the ordained priest. We too frequently
   forget this dignity of baptism.
5. Gregory of Nyssa.

5. Obedience in the Bible

1. The ecumenical spirit of our times is easily scandalised by the
   vehemence of this chapter. We cannot annul it, on the pretext of
   the polemic between the Church and Synagogue of the first centuries. The conflict was real and the consequences tragic. Here,
   Jesus is placing himself in the tradition of the great prophets who
   were no easier than he on the deformations of Jewish piety.
2. On this point see the quotation from Karl Rahner at the end of
   this conference.

6. Obedience in St John

1. Fr. *disponibilité*.

7. Obedience in St Paul and the Letter to the Hebrews

1. Do not despise the letter: 'Without the letter, the spirit is not the spirit' (Blondel).
2. See the beautiful texts: 2:17–18; 4:14–16; 10:19–23.
3. Ministerial priesthood is situated along another line, that of a certain service within the Body of Christ.

8. Obedience in the Desert Fathers

1. A Semitism to express 'without preferring me to'. See Matthew 10:37–9.
2. See S.P. Brock, *The Luminous Eye* (Kalamazoo: Cistercian, 1992), pp. 131ff.
3. Cassian, *Conferences*, II, 24.
4. For example, *The Sayings of the Desert Fathers, The Alphabetical Collection*, tr. Benedicta Ward (London: Mowbray, revised edition 1981); *The Wisdom of the Desert Fathers*, tr. Benedicta Ward (Oxford: SLG Press, 1981); *The World of the Desert Fathers*, tr. Columba Stewart (Oxford: Fairacres, 1986); *The Ladder of Divine Ascent* by John Climacus, 4th step.
5. Cassian, *Institutes*, 4,8.
6. Poemen, 54, in Ward, p. 174.
7. John Climacus, *The Ladder of Divine Ascent*, step 4,3, tr. Colin Luibheid and Norman Russell, The Classics of Western Spirituality (New York: Paulist Press, 1982), p. 92.
8. Syncletica, 16, in Ward, p. 234.
9. John the Dwarf, 1, in Ward, p. 85.
10. Mark, 1, in Ward, pp. 145–6.
11. Hyperechius, 8, in Ward, p. 239.

9. Obedience in Monasteries

1. Translation of the sections from the *Rule of St Benedict* by Anthony C. Meisel and M.L. del Mastro (Garden City, New York: Image Books, 1975).

2. Treatise cited by M. Olphe-Gaillard in *L'Obéissance et la Religieuse d'aujourd'hui*, p. 29.

3. Cassian is the origin for these degrees.

10. Evolution of the Practice of Obedience

1. To the extent that it is conformed to the ordering of God. We must not stretch this thesis to canonise every authority, even the most unjust and immoral. See John 19:11; 1 Peter 2:13; Titus 3:1; Romans 13:1: 'Let every person be subject to the governing authorities; for there is no authority except from God, and those authorities that exist have been instituted by God.'

2. The hierarchical structure is also open to the work of the Spirit. The superior has received the grace of the Order and he has the grace of office to help him worthily fulfil his function which should usually be the case. But his personal value is not the source of his authority.

3. This is above all true in that which concerns our personal life: no one is a good judge for his own situation.

4. Obviously this is impossible if what is commanded is contrary to moral law; when serious damage to the interests of third parties are in question, there can arise a complex case of conscience.

5. Fr.: *disponible*.

12. Obedience According to the Decree *Perfectae Caritatis* II

1. 'Freedom is a natural and inalienable endowment of human beings, in so far as they are beings gifted with reason, capable of discerning moral values, called by God to aspire to a goal by making use of personal choices which are only valid when they are made spontaneously whereas any order forced on a person, without the free consent of the will, would strip these choices of their human and religious significance' (Cardinal Pelligrino, *Le Problème de l'Obéissance* (Paris: Apost. des Éditions, 1969)), p. 201.

2. D.H. = *Dignitatis Humanae*, the decree on religious liberty.

3. G.S. = *Gaudium et Spes*, the decree on the Church in the modern world.

4. O.T. = *Optatam Totius*, the decree on the training of priests.

13. Obedience in the Renewed Statutes

1. ' . . .ad eum per oboedientiae laborem redeant, a quo per inoboedientia desidiam homo recesserat', p. 550.

2. Fr. *disponibilité*.

3. *The Meditations of Guigo I, Prior of the Charterhouse*, tr. A. Gordon Mursell, Cistercian Studies Series, no. 155 (Kalamazoo, 1995), p. 65.

4. 'The true spirit of the Order does not at all consist in a certain obstinate asperity of austerity, but in the practice of fulfilling the Statutes, according to charity, meekness, humility and the evangelical counsels, which are the foundations of Carthusian life, to which all the rest should be related and without which everything else counts for nothing at all' (Dom Innocent Le Masson, *Direction et Sujets de Méditation pour les Retraites* (Montreuil-sur-Mer: Imprimerie Notre-Dame des Prés, 1890), pp. 218–19).

5. Furthermore, the whole network of controls: the Prior General, Visitors, General Chapter guarantee that the Prior's governance remains along the line of our vocation.

6. A. Gordon Mursell, op. cit., p. 161.

7. Ibid., p. 175.

8. A good example is the responsible, personal attitude in regard to corporal penance described in 1.7.3.

9. I do not in any way exclude the real contribution of each person and every era to the tradition, but the attitude – at bottom, pride – that oneself alone is the measure of everything.

15. Contemplative Obedience

1. Fr. *disponibilité*.

16. Authority in the Gospel

1. (Fr. 'Master'.) Let us note that in verse 8 the prohibition on having oneself called 'Master' is limited to the disciples; because they call Christ 'Master' and he accepts being called 'Master' (which is not the case for 'Father': we will return to this question in an

Appendix). The disciples grouped around the Master are all brothers (Gk. 'brothers' instead of the English 'students'). But when the Master disappears, the one who represents him among the disciples can be called 'master' without contradicting his word. But it is more evangelical among us to call ourselves 'brothers'.

2. It is the mother who asks but it would seem that it is the sons who ask through her, as intermediary, as Jesus replies directly to them.

17. Authority in Peter and Paul

1. See the qualities of ministers of God in 2 Corinthians 6:3–11.

18. Spiritual Fatherhood

1. It seems that it would be forcing Jesus' thought to interpret this in the sense of a negation of every relationship of fatherhood outside the divine fatherhood. Semitic thought expresses the relative in absolute terms ('hate your father and mother' Luke 14:26; 'whoever does the will of God is my brother, my sister, my mother' Mark 3:35). Jesus affirms that divine fatherhood is the transcendent source of all human fatherhood; if we stop here as if this were a reality in itself, it can be an obstacle instead of being a sacrament and an image. The thought of the first monks runs along this line: they frequently affirm that spiritual parenting which gives birth to the life of the Spirit is far superior to merely 'fleshly' parenting and closer to that of God.

2. St John doesn't hesitate to call adult members of the Christian community 'father' (1 John 2:13–14).

3. I admit I am a little uneasy in regard to this explanation.

4. As in God, spiritual fecundity encompasses fatherly and motherly characteristics. When it is a question of women, we speak of spiritual maternity to designate this reality. And history offers many examples of women who 'having left the world serve God with children engendered through them according to Christ' (Oriental text).

5. Every spiritual person, in so much as he helps a brother, even as merely a simple and fraternal presence, is participating in the fatherhood, of which superiors do not have a monopoly.

6. Let us note that the hierarchical superiors of the monastery are not automatically spiritual people; at the same time, ordinarily, we

should find in them two sources of the Spirit: a personal spiritual life for which reason they were elected, and 'the grace of office', that is to say, the help of the Spirit in their ecclesial charge. The structure of the Church is also animated by the Spirit; but the Spirit acts through free persons, who are more or less faithful to his grace. Solomon began well. A continual renewal of faith and docility is required from superiors.

19. Authority in the Church

1. Fr. disponibilité.

20. Authority According to the Statutes

1. A. Gordon Mursell, op.cit., p. 91.
2. Ibid., p. 128.
3. Gk. fatherhood.
4. *Antiqua Statuta*, Ch. V, no. 3.
5. First included in the 1924 Statutes.
6. See also Ch. 20 'The Formation of the Brothers'.

21. Notes on the Responsibilities of Superiors According to Group Psychology

1. These notes are taken, frequently literally, from the book by André de Perretti, *Liberté et Relations humaines ou l'Inspiration Non-Directive* (Paris: Épi, 1972), pp. 109ff.
2. Another image: the stove (the superior) – too close, you get burned, too far, you freeze.
3. Recall the emotional resonances evoked by the word 'father' and the transference onto the person who is in a position of authority, of experiences of conflict which have not been resolved.

22. The Father Master of Novices in the History of Chartreuse

1. The historical information given is only a resumé of the meticulous research made by Dom Maurice Laporte.
2. From this point on we are speaking only of the Grande Chartreuse, the only house for which there is documentation in hand.